RUSSIAN

in 10 minutes a day®

by Kristine Kershul, M.A., University of California, Santa Barbara

Consultants: **Kamal Bouranov**   **Alla A. Smyslova**
              Marianna Ilyina

Bilingual Books, Inc.

1719 West Nickerson Street, Seattle, WA 98119
Tel: (206) 284-4211 Fax: (206) 284-3660
www.10minutesaday.com • www.bbks.com

ISBN-13: 978-1-931873-10-9   First printing, November 2008

Can you say this?

(shtoh) *(et-tah)*
Что это?
what (is)   that

(et-tah) *(soop)*
Это суп.
that (is)   soup

(yah) *(hah-choo)* *(soo-pah)*
Я хочу супа.
I   would like   soup

If you can say this, you can learn to speak Russian. You will be able to easily order Russian tea, vodka, ballet tickets, caviar, pastry, or anything else you wish. You simply ask **"Что это?"** *(shtoh)(et-tah)* and, upon learning what it is, you can order it with **"Я хочу этого"** *(yah) (hah-choo) (et-tah-vah)*. Sounds easy, doesn't it?

The purpose of this book is to give you an **immediate** speaking ability in Russian. When you first see Russian words, they can appear to be forbidding. However, they are not when you know how to decode and pronounce these new letters. This book offers above each word a unique and easy system of pronunciation which walks you through learning Russian.

If you are planning a trip or moving to where Russian is spoken, you will be leaps ahead of everyone if you take just a few minutes a day to learn the easy key words that this book offers. Start with Step 1 and don't skip around. Each day work as far as you can comfortably go in those 10 minutes. Don't overdo it. Some days you might want to just review. If you forget a word, you can always look it up in the glossary. Spend your first 10 minutes studying the map on the previous page. And yes, have fun learning your new language.

As you work through the Steps, always use the special features which only this Series offers. This book contains sticky labels and flash cards, free words, puzzles, and quizzes. When you have completed the book, cut out the menu guide and take it along on your trip.

(ahl-fah-veet)
Алфавит
alphabet

Above all new words is an easy pronunciation guide. Refer to this Step whenever you need help, but remember, spend no longer than 10 minutes a day. Here are five Russian letters which look and sound like English.

(ah)	*(k)*	*(m)*	*(oh or ah)*	*(t)*
а	**к**	**м**	**о**	**т**

Russian has seven letters which look like English, but be careful; they are not pronounced like English.

(v)	*(eh or yeh)*	*(n)*	*(r)*	*(s)*	*(oo)*	*(h or hk)*
в	**е**	**н**	**р**	**с**	**у**	**х**

The following Russian letters look quite different from English. They are easy to pronounce once you decode them. Practice writing out the individual letters to the best of your ability. Are you ready?

(b)	*(g)*	*(d)*	*(yoh)*	*(zh)*	*(z)*	*(ee)*	*(varies, see list)*	*(l)*	*(p)*
б	**г**	**д**	**ё**	**ж**	**з**	**и**	**й**	**л**	**п**

Г, Г

(f)	*(ts)*	*(ch or sh)*	*(sh)*	*(shch)*	*(ih or ee)*	*(eh)*	*(yoo)*	*(yah)*
ф	**ц**	**ч**	**ш**	**щ**	**ы**	**э**	**ю**	**я**

Я, Я

Here is the entire Russian alphabet in **Russian** alphabetical order for quick reference. Practice these new letters and sounds with the examples given which are mostly Russian first names. A black underline indicates a man's name and a blue underline is for a woman's.

Russian letter	**English sound**	**Example**	*Write it here*
а	ah	**Анна** *(ahn-nah)*	Анна, Анна, Анна
б	b	**Борис** *(bahr-ees)*	Борис, Борис, Борис
в	v	**Вадим** *(vah-deem)*	Вадим
г	g (or v)	**Глеб** *(gleb)*	Глеб, Глеб
д	d	**Дмитрий** *(dmee-tree)*	
е	eh *(as in let)* yeh *(as in yet)*	**Елена** *(eh-lyen-ah)*	
ё	yoh	**Фёдор** *(fyoh-dor)*	

ж	zh	**Жанна** (*zhahn-nah*)	_____
з	z	**Зина** (*zee-nah*)	_____
и	ee	**Никита** (*nee-kee-tah*)	_____
й (*varies*)	oy / ay / i / ee	**Майя** (*my-yah*)	_____
к	k	**Катя** (*kaht-yah*)	_____
л	l	**Лариса** (*lah-ree-sah*)	_____
м	m	**Максим** (*mahk-seem*)	_____
н	n	**Николай** (*nee-kah-lie*)	_____
о (*varies*)	oh	**Ольга** (*ohl-gah*)	_____
	ah	**Полина** (*pah-lee-nah*)	_____
п	p	**Паша** (*pah-shah*)	_____
р	r	**Рина** (*ree-nah*)	_____
с	s	**Сергей** (*syair-gay*)	_____
т	t	**Татьяна** (*taht-yah-nah*)	_____
у	oo	**Эдуард** (*ed-oo-ard*)	_____
ф	f	**Софья** (*sohf-yah*)	_____
х	h / hk	**Михаил** (*mee-hah-eel*)	_____
ц	ts (*as in cats*)	**Царёв** (*tsar-yohv*)	_____
ч	ch / sh	**Вячеслав** (*vyah-cheh-slahv*)	_____
ш	sh	**Саша** (*sah-shah*)	_____
щ (*varies*)	shch / sh	**Щукин** (*shchoo-keen*)	_____
ъ	no sound, called a hard sign, a word divider		
ы (*varies*)	ih / ee	**Рыбаков** (*rih-bah-kohv*)	_____
ь	no sound, called a soft sign, a word divider		
э (*varies*)	eh	**Элла** (*el-lah*)	_____
ю	yoo	**Юрий** (*yoor-ee*)	_____
я	yah	**Юлия** (*yool-ee-yah*)	_____

By now you should have a reasonable grasp on the Russian alphabet. Letters can change their pronunciation depending upon whether they are stressed or unstressed. Take the letter **о.** It is pronounced "*oh*" when stressed and "*ah*" otherwise. Don't worry about it, you'll learn!

Sometimes the phonetics may seem to contradict your pronunciation guide. Don't panic! The easiest and best-possible phonetics have been chosen for each individual word. Pronounce the phonetics just as you see them. Don't over-analyze them. Speak with a Russian accent and, above all, enjoy yourself!

When you arrive in **Россию,** *(rahs-see-yoo)* Russia the very first thing you will need to do is ask questions — "Where is the bus stop?" "Where can I exchange money?" "Where (**где**) *(gdyeh)* is the lavatory?" "**Где** *(gdyeh)* is a restaurant?" "**Где** *(gdyeh)* do I catch a taxi?" "**Где** *(gdyeh)* is a good hotel?" "**Где** *(gdyeh)* where is my luggage?" — and the list will go on and on for the entire length of your visit. In Russian, there are SEVEN KEY QUESTION WORDS to learn. For example, the seven key question words will help you find out exactly what you are ordering in a restaurant before you order it — and not after the surprise (or shock!) arrives. Notice that "what" and "who" are differentiated by only one letter, so be sure not to confuse them. Take a few minutes to study and practice saying the seven basic question words listed below. Then cover the **русский** *(roos-skee)* Russian with your hand and fill in each of the blanks with the matching **русским** *(roos-skeem)* Russian **словом.** *(slah-vahm)* word

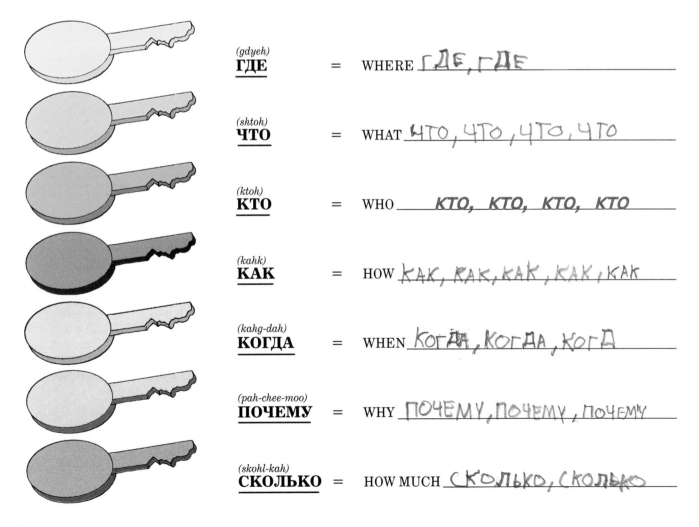

ГДЕ *(gdyeh)*   =   WHERE   ГДЕ, ГДЕ

ЧТО *(shtoh)*   =   WHAT   ЧТО, ЧТО, ЧТО, ЧТО

КТО *(ktoh)*   =   WHO   КТО, КТО, КТО, КТО

КАК *(kahk)*   =   HOW   КАК, КАК, КАК, КАК, КАК

КОГДА *(kahg-dah)*   =   WHEN   КОГДА, КОГДА, КОГД

ПОЧЕМУ *(pah-chee-moo)*   =   WHY   ПОЧЕМУ, ПОЧЕМУ, ПОЧЕМУ

СКОЛЬКО *(skohl-kah)*   =   HOW MUCH   СКОЛЬКО, СКОЛЬКО

Now test yourself to see if you really can keep these **слова** *(slah-vah)* / words straight in your mind. Draw lines between the **русскими** *(roos-skee-mee)* / Russian **и** *(ee)* / and English equivalents below.

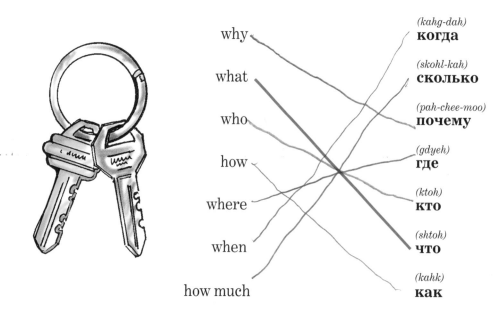

why — **когда** *(kahg-dah)*

what — **сколько** *(skohl-kah)*

who — **почему** *(pah-chee-moo)*

how — **где** *(gdyeh)*

where — **кто** *(ktoh)*

when — **что** *(shtoh)*

how much — **как** *(kahk)*

Examine the following questions containing these words. Practice the sentences out loud **и** *(ee)* / and then practice by copying the Russian in the blanks underneath each question.

Что это? *(shtoh) (et-tah)*
what (is)   that?

Что это? Что это?

Где салат? *(gdyeh) (sah-laht)*
where (is) the salad

Кто это? *(ktoh) (et-tah)*
who (is)   that?

Кто это? Кто это?

Когда балет? *(kahg-dah) (bahl-yet)*
when (is)   the ballet

Когда балет?

Сколько это стоит? *(skohl-kah) (et-tah) (stoy-eet)*
how much (does) that cost

Сколько это стоит? Сколько это стоит?

Как дела? *(kahk) (dee-lah)*
how are things / how are you

Как дела? Как дела?

"**Где**" *(gdyeh)* / where will be your most used question **слово** *(sloh-vah)* / word. Say each of the following **русские** *(roos-skee-yeh)* / Russian sentences aloud. Then write out each sentence without looking at the example. If you don't succeed on the first try, don't give up. Just practice each sentence until you are able to do it easily. Remember "**c**" is pronounced like an "s" **и** *(ee)* "**p**" is pronounced like an "r."

(gdyeh) (too-ahl-yet)
Где туалет?
where (is) a toilet

(gdyeh) (tahk-see)
Где такси?
where (is) a taxi

(gdyeh) (ahv-toh-boos)
Где автобус?
where (is) a bus

Где туалет?

ГДеТакси? ГДе Такси?

ГДе автобус? ГДе автобус?

(gdyeh) (res-tah-rahn)
Где ресторан?
a restaurant

(bahnk)
Где банк?
a bank

(gah-stee-neet-sah)
Где гостиница?
a hotel / an inn

ГДе ресторан? ГДе ресторан? Где банк? Где банк?

ГДе Гостиница?

(dah)
Да, you can see similarities between **русским и английским,** if you look closely. **Русский**
yes   *(roos-skeem)* *(ee)* *(ahn-glee-skeem)*   *(roos-skee)*
                                                                                                          Russian   English

(ahn-glee-skee)
и английский are not related languages, but some words are surprisingly similar. Of course,
and

they do not always sound the same when spoken by a Russian, but the similarities will

certainly surprise you and make your work here easier. Listed below are five "free" **слов**
                                                                                                                          (slohv)
                                                                                                                          words

beginning with **"а"** to help you get started. Be sure to say each **слово** aloud **и** then write out
        (ah)   *(sloh-vah)*   *(ee)*

(roos-skah-yeh) (sloh-vah)
the **русское слово** in the blank to the right.
Russian   word

☐ **абрикос** *(ah-bree-kohs)*	apricot	аб рикос, абрикос, абрикос
☐ **август** *(ahv-goost)*	August	август, август, август, август
☐ **авиация** *(ah-vee-aht-see-yah)*	aviation	**а** авиация, авиация, авиация
☐ **Австралия** *(ahv-strah-lee-yah)*	Australia	австралия, австралия, австралия
☐ **Австрия** *(ahv-stree-yah)*	Austria	австрия, австрия, австрия австрия

(slah-vah)
Free **слова** like these will appear at the bottom of the following pages in a yellow color band.
words

They are easy — enjoy them! Don't forget to pronounce **"и"** as "ee."

(roos-skee) (yah-zik)
Русский язык does not have *(slohv)* **слов** for "the" and "a," which makes things easier for you.
Russian   language   words

(slah-vah)
Russian **слова** also change their endings depending upon how they are used, so don't be
words

(slah-vah)
surprised! Learn **слова** and be prepared to see their endings change. Here are some examples.
the words

(sloh-vah)
слово
word

(slah-vah)
слова

(sloh-voo)
слову

(sloh-vahm)
словом

(slohv)
слов

(slah-vah-mee)
словами

(kuh-nee-gah)
книга
book

(kuh-nee-gee)
книги

(kuh-nee-geh)
книге

(kuh-nee-goo)
книгу

(kuh-nee-goy)
книгой

(kuh-neeg)
книг

(stool)
стул
chair

(stool-ah)
стула

(stool-oo)
стулу

(stool-ohm)
стулом

(stool-yeh)
стуле

(stool-yah)
стулья

(ahn-glee-skah-vah) (yah-zih-kah)
This only appears difficult because it is different from **английского языка.** Just remember
English   language

(sloh-vah)
the core of **слова** doesn't change, so you should always be able to recognize it. For instance,
the word

(kuh-nee-gah) (kuh-nee-goo)
you will be understood whether you say **книга** or **книгу.** Learn to look and listen for the
book

core of the word, and don't worry about the different endings.

In Step 2 you were introduced to the Seven Key QuestionWords. These seven words are the basics, the most essential building blocks for learning Russian. Throughout this book you will come across keys asking you to fill in the missing question word. Use this opportunity not only to fill in the blank on that key, but to review all your question words. Play with the new sounds, speak slowly and have fun.

❏ **автобиография** *(ahv-tah-bee-ah-grah-fee-yah)* . . autobiography _____
❏ **автограф** *(ahv-toh-grahf)* . . . . autograph _____
❏ **автомат** *(ahv-tah-maht)* . . . . automat **a** _____
❏ **автомобиль** *(ahv-tah-mah-beel)* . . . . automobile _____
❏ **автор** *(ahv-tar)* . . . . author _____

Before you proceed with this Step, situate yourself comfortably in your living room. Now look

around you. Can you name the things that you see in this **комнате** *(kohm-nah-tyeh)* in Russian? You can
room

probably guess **лампа** *(lahm-pah)* and maybe even **диван.** *(dee-vahn)* But let's learn the rest of them. After
lamp   divan / sofa

practicing these **слова** *(slah-vah)* out loud, write them in the blanks below.
words

(lahm-pah)
лампа   Лампа, Лампа, Лампа, Лампа,
lamp / light

(dee-vahn)
диван   Диван, Диван, Диван, Диван
sofa

(stool)
стул   Стул, Стул, Стул, Стул, Стул, Стул, Стул
chair

(kahv-yor)
ковёр   ковёр, ковёр
carpet

(stohl)
стол   Стол, Стол, Стол, Стол
table

(dvyair)
дверь   Дверь, Дверь, Дверь, Дверь, Дверь, Дверь
door

(chah-sih)
часы   Часы, Часы, Часы, Часы, Часы, Часы, Часы
clock

(zah-nahv-yes)
занавес   Занавес, Занавес, Занавес, Занавес
curtain

(teh-leh-fohn)
телефон   Телефон, Телефон, Телефон
telephone

(ahk-noh)
окно
window
ОКНО, ОКНО, ОКНО

(kar-tee-nah)
картина
picture

Картина, Картина, Картина, Картина

In Step 3, you learned that **русские** *(roos-skee-yeh)* **слова** *(slah-vah)* vary. The correct form of each **слова** *(sloh-vah)* will always
Russian   words   word

be given to familiarize you with the variations. Now open your **книгу** *(kuh-nee-goo)* to the sticky labels on
book

page 17 and later on page 35. Peel off the first 11 labels **и** *(ee)* proceed around your **комнаты** *(kohm-nah-tih)*
and   room

labeling these items in your home. This will help to increase your **русское** *(roos-skah-yeh)* **слово** *(sloh-vah)* power
Russian   word

easily. Don't forget to say each **слово** *(sloh-vah)* as you attach each label.
word

Now ask yourself, "**Где** *(gdyeh)* **лампа?**" *(lahm-pah)* and point at it while you answer, "**Там** *(tahm)* **лампа.**" *(lahm-pah)*
                 the lamp   there is   the lamp

Continue on down the list above until you feel comfortable with these new **словами.** *(slah-vah-mee)*
words

❏ **агент** *(ah-gyent)*	agent	_____
❏ **адвокат** *(ahd-vah-kaht)*	advocate, lawyer	_____
❏ **адрес** *(ah-dres)*	address	**a** _____
❏ **Азия** *(ah-zee-yah)*	Asia	_____
❏ **академия** *(ah-kah-dyeh-mee-yah)*	academy	_____

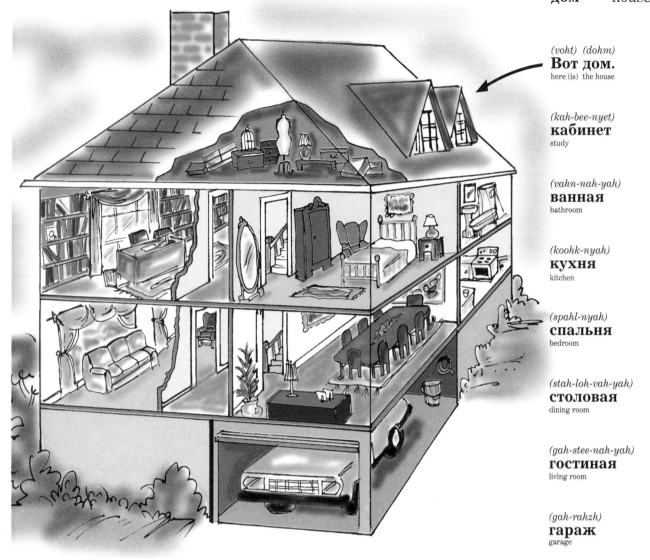

(dohm)
дом = house

(voht) (dohm)
Вот дом.
here (is) the house

(kah-bee-nyet)
кабинет
study

(vahn-nah-yah)
ванная
bathroom

(koohk-nyah)
кухня
kitchen

(spahl-nyah)
спальня
bedroom

(stah-loh-vah-yah)
столовая
dining room

(gah-stee-nah-yah)
гостиная
living room

(gah-rahzh)
гараж
garage

(pahd-vahl)
подвал
basement

(slah-vah)
While learning these new **слова,** let's not forget:
words

(ahv-tah-mah-beel) *(mah-shee-nah)*
автомобиль / машина
automobile / car

_____

(mah-tah-tsee-kul)
мотоцикл
motorcycle

_____

(vyeh-lah-see-pyed)
велосипед
bicycle

_____

❏ **аккуратный** *(ahk-koo-raht-nee)*	fastidious, neat, accurate		_____
❏ **акробат** *(ah-krah-baht)*	acrobat		_____
❏ **акт** *(ahkt)*	act	**а**	_____
❏ **актёр** *(ahk-tyor)*	actor		_____
❏ **акцент** *(ahkt-syent)*	accent		_____

(kohsh-kah)
кошка
cat

(sahd)
сад
garden

(tsvet-ih)
цветы
flowers

_____   *сад, сад, сад*   _____

(sah-bah-kah)
собака
dog

(pahch-toh-vee) (yahsh-chik)
почтовый ящик
mailbox

(poach-tah)
почта
mail

_____   _____   _____

Peel off the next set of labels **и** *(ee)* wander through your **дом** *(dohm)* learning these new **слова**. *(slah-vah)* words It will

be somewhat difficult to label your **кошку**, *(kohsh-koo)* cat **цветы** *(tsvet-ih)* flowers or **собаку**, *(sah-bah-koo)* dog but be creative. Practice by

asking yourself, **"Где машина?"** *(gdyeh) (mah-shee-nah)* the car and reply, **"Вот машина." "Где дом?"** *(voht) (mah-shee-nah) (gdyeh)* here (is)

☐ **алгебра** *(ahl-gyeh-brah)*	algebra	_____
☐ **алкоголь** *(ahl-kah-gohl)*	alcohol, alcoholic drinks	_____
☐ **Америка** *(ah-myeh-ree-kah)*	America	_____
☐ — **американец** *(ah-myeh-ree-kah-nyets)* . . .	American male	_____
☐ — **американка** *(ah-myeh-ree-kahn-kah)*	American female	_____

а

11

Один, два, три

(ah-deen) *(dvah)* *(tree)*
one   two   three

Consider for a minute how important numbers are. How could you tell someone your phone

number, your address **или** *(ee-lee)* your hotel room if you had no numbers? And think of how difficult

or

if would be if you could not understand the time, the price of an apple **или** *(ee-lee)* the correct bus to

or

take. When practicing **числа** *(chee-slah)* below, notice the similarities which have been underlined for you

numbers

between **один** *(ah-deen)* and **одиннадцать,** *(ah-deen-nud-tset)* **три** *(tree)* and **тринадцать,** *(tree-nahd-tset)* and so on.

one   eleven   three   thirteen

0	*(nohl)* **ноль**	Ноль, Ноль, Ноль, Ноль, Ноль	**10**	*(dyes-yet)* **десять**	Десять, Десять, Десять
1	*(ah-deen)* **один**	Один, Один, Один, Один	**11**	*(ah-deen-nud-tset)* **одиннадцать**	Одиннадцет
2	*(dvah) (dveh)* **два/ две**	Два, два, Два, Два, Два	**12**	*(dveh-nahd-tset)* **двенадцать**	Двенадцать
3	*(tree)* **три**	Три, Три, Три, Три, Три, Три	**13**	*(tree-nahd-tset)* **тринадцать**	
4	*(cheh-tir-ee)* **четыре**	Четыре, Четыре, Четыре	**14**	*(cheh-tir-nud-tset)* **четырнадцать**	
5	*(pyaht)* **пять**	пять, пять, пять, пять, пять, пять	**15**	*(pyaht-nahd-tset)* **пятнадцать**	
6	*(shest)* **шесть**	шесть, Шесть, шесть, шесть	**16**	*(shest-nahd-tset)* **шестнадцать**	
7	*(syem)* **семь**	*семь, семь, семь*	**17**	*(sim-nahd-tset)* **семнадцать**	
8	*(voh-syem)* **восемь**	Восемь, Восемь, Восемь	**18**	*(vah-sim-nahd-tset)* **восемнадцать**	
9	*(dyev-yet)* **девять**	Девять, Девять, девять,	**19**	*(div-yet-nahd-tset)* **девятнадцать**	
10	*(dyes-yet)* **десять**	Десять, Десять, Десять	**20**	*(dvahd-tset)* **двадцать**	

❏ **алло!** *(ahl-loh)*	hello!
❏ **Англия** *(ahn-glee-yah)*	England
❏ — where they speak **по-английски** *(pah-ahn-glee-skee)*	
❏ — **англичанин** *(ahn-glee-chah-neen)*	Englishman
❏ — **англичанка** *(ahn-glee-chahn-kah)*	Englishwoman

а

Use these **числа** *(chee-slah)* on a daily basis. Count to yourself **по-русски** *(pah-roos-skee)* when you brush your teeth,

numbers   in   Russian

exercise **или** *(ee-lee)* commute to work. Fill in the blanks below according to **числам** *(chee-slahm)* given in

or   numbers

parentheses. Now is also a good time to learn these two **очень** *(oh-chen)* important phrases.

very

(yah) *(hah-choo)* *(koo-peet)*
Я ХОЧУ КУПИТЬ Я хочу купить, Я хочу купить, Я хочу купить, Я хочу
I   would like   to buy

(mwee) *(hah-teem)* *(koo-peet)*
МЫ ХОТИМ КУПИТЬ Мы хотим купит, Мы хотим купит, Мы хотим купить
we   would like   to buy

(yah) *(hah-choo)* *(koo-peet)*
Я ХОЧУ КУПИТЬ ОДИН (1)   **открытку.** *(aht-krit-koo)*   **Сколько?** *(skohl-kah)* один (1)
I   would like   to buy   postcard   how many / how much

(hah-choo) *(koo-peet)*
Я ХОЧУ КУПИТЬ семь (7)   **марок.** *(mar-ahk)*   **Сколько?** *(skohl-kah)* семь (7)
I   would like   stamps

(hah-choo) *(koo-peet)*
Я ХОЧУ КУПИТЬ восемь (8)   **марок.** *(mar-ahk)*   **Сколько?** *(skohl-kah)* восемь (8)
                      stamps

(hah-choo) *(koo-peet)*
Я ХОЧУ КУПИТЬ пять (5)   **марок.**   **Сколько?** *(skohl-kah)* пять (5)
                                       how many

(mwee) *(hah-teem)* *(koo-peet)*
Мы ХОТИМ КУПИТЬ девять (9)   **открыток.** *(aht-krih-tahk)*   **Сколько?** *(skohl-kah)* девять (9)
we   would like   to buy   postcards

(mwee) *(hah-teem)*
Мы ХОТИМ КУПИТЬ десять (10)   **открыток.** *(aht-krih-tahk)*   **Сколько?** *(skohl-kah)* десять (10)
we   would like   postcards

(yah) *(hah-choo)*
Я ХОЧУ КУПИТЬ один (1)   **билет.** *(beel-yet)*   **Сколько?** *(skohl-kah)* один (1)
I   would like   ticket

(mwee) *(hah-teem)*
Мы ХОТИМ КУПИТЬ четыре (4)   **билета.** *(beel-yet-ah)*   **Сколько?** *(skohl-kah)* четыре (4)
we   would like   tickets

(hah-teem)
Мы ХОТИМ КУПИТЬ (11)   **билетов.** *(beel-yet-ahv)*   **Сколько?** (11)
    would like

(yah) *(hah-teem)*
Я ХОЧУ КУПИТЬ три (3)   **чашки чая.** *(chahsh-kee)* *(chah-yah)*   **Сколько?** три (3)
                       cups of   tea

(hah-teem)
Мы ХОТИМ КУПИТЬ четыре (4)   **чашки кофе.** *(chahsh-kee)* *(koh-fyeh)*   **Сколько?** *(how much)* четыри (4)
                       cups of   coffee

❏ **анекдот** *(ah-nyek-doht)* .... anecdote, joke
❏ **антенна** *(ahn-tyen-nah)* .... antenna
❏ **антибиотики** *(ahn-tee-bee-oh-tee-kee)* ...... antibiotics   **a**
❏ **аппетит** *(ah-peh-teet)* .... appetite
❏ **апрель** *(ahp-ryel)* .... April

13

Now see if you can translate the following thoughts **на** **русский.** **Ответы** are provided upside

(nah) *(roos-skee)* *(aht-vyet-ih)*
into *Russian* *the answers*

down at the bottom of the page.

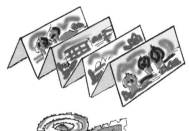

1. I would like to buy seven postcards.

Я хочу купить семь открыток

2. I would like to buy nine stamps.

Я хочу купить девять марок

3. We would like to buy four cups of tea.

Мы хотим купить четыре чашки чая

4. We would like to buy three tickets.

Мы хотим купить три билета

Review **числа** 1 through 20. Write out your telephone number, fax number, and cellular

(chee-slah)
numbers

number. Then write out a friend's telephone number and then a relative's telephone number.

(2 0 6) 2 8 4 — 4 2 1 1

два ноль шесть

(4 2 5) 2 3 8 — 3 1 8 1

Четыре два пять два три восемь три один восемь один

( ) —

_____

ОТВЕТЫ

14

(tsvet-ah)
Цвета
colors

(tsvet-ah)   *(pah-roos-skee)*   *(pah-ahn-glee-skee)*   *(ee-myen-ah)*

Цвета are the same **по-русски** as they are **по-английски** — they just have different **имена.**
colors   in   Russian   in   English   names

                            (tsvet)   *(sah-vyet-skahm)*   *(sah-yoo-zeh)*   *(tsvet-ah)*   *(rahs-see-skah-vah)*

Red used to be the national **цвет** in **Советском Союзе.** **Цвета** of the new **российского**
                            color   Soviet   Union   colors   Russian

      (byeh-lee)   *(gah-loo-boy)*   *(krahs-nee)*   *(tsvet-ah)*

flag are — **белый, голубой и красный.** Let's learn the basic **цвета.** Once you've learned
         white   light blue   red   colors

(tsvet-ah)

цвета, quiz yourself. What color are your shoes? Your eyes? Your hair? Your house?
the colors

(roh-zah-vwee)
розовый
pink
<u>розовый, розовый</u>

(krahs-nee)
красный
red
<u>Красный, красный</u>

(ah-rahn-zheh-vwee)
оранжевый
orange
<u>оранжевый, оранжевый</u>

(byeh-lee)
белый
white
<u>белый, белый, белый</u>

(see-nee)
синий
blue
<u>синий, синий, синий</u>

(syeh-ree)
серый
gray
<u>серый, серый, серый</u>

(zhyol-tee)
жёлтый
yellow
<u>жёлтый, жёлтый, жёлтый</u>

(kah-reech-nyeh-vwee)
коричневый
brown
<u>коричневый</u>

(zyel-yoh-nee)
зелёный
green
<u>зелёный, зелёный, зелёный</u>

(chyor-nee)
чёрный
black
<u>чёрный, чёрный, чёрный</u>

(gah-loo-boy)
голубой
light blue
<u>голубой, голубой, голубой</u>

❏ **арена** *(ar-yen-ah)* . . . . arena

❏ **арест** *(ar-yest)* . . . . arrest

❏ **армия** *(ar-mee-yah)* . . . . army   **а**

❏ **аспирин** *(ah-spee-reen)* . . . . aspirin

❏ **астронавт** *(ah-strah-nahvt)* . . . . astronaut

Peel off the next group of labels **и** proceed to label these *(tsvet-ah)* **цвета** *(vuh)* **в** your *(doh-myeh)* **доме.** Identify the
colors in house

two or three dominant colors in the flags below.

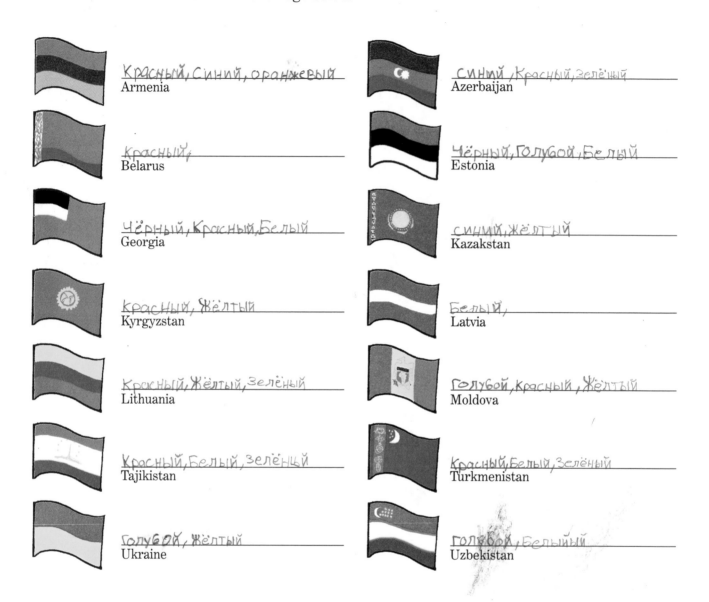

Armenia — Красный, Синий, оранжевый

Azerbaijan — Синий, Красный, зелёный

Belarus — Красный,

Estonia — Чёрный, Голубой, Белый

Georgia — Чёрный, Красный, Белый

Kazakstan — Синий, жёлтый

Kyrgyzstan — Красный, Жёлтый

Latvia — Белый,

Lithuania — Красный, Жёлтый, зелёный

Moldova — Голубой, Красный, Жёлтый

Tajikistan — Красный, Белый, зелёный

Turkmenistan — Красный, Белый, Зелёный

Ukraine — Голубой, Жёлтый

Uzbekistan — голубой, Белый

You should be able to use your **русский** language skills in any of the above countries. Kyrgyz

may be the official language of Kyrgyzstan, but **русский** may be more commonly used

и understood.

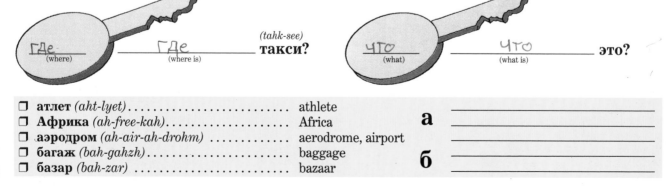

Где (where) ___ Где ___ (where is) *(tahk-see)* **такси?**

Что (what) ___ Что ___ (what is) **это?**

□ **атлет** *(aht-lyet)* . . . . athlete
□ **Африка** *(ah-free-kah)* . . . . Africa   **а** ___
□ **аэродром** *(ah-air-ah-drohm)* . . . . aerodrome, airport
□ **багаж** *(bah-gahzh)* . . . . baggage   **б** ___
□ **базар** *(bah-zar)* . . . . bazaar

(ahv-tah-mah-beel)
автомобиль

(mah-tah-tsee-kul)
мотоцикл

(mah-lah-koh)
молоко

(krahs-nee)
красный

(mah-slah)
масло

(roh-zah-vwee)
розовый

(sole)
соль

(kahv-yor)
ковёр

(kohsh-kah)
кошка

(ah-rahn-zheh-vwee)
оранжевый

(pyeh-rets)
перец

(sahd)
сад

(byeh-lee)
белый

(bah-kahl)
бокал

(tsvet-ih)
цветы

(zhyol-tee)
жёлтый

(stah-kahn)
стакан

(chah-sih)
часы

(sah-bah-kah)
собака

(syeh-ree)
серый

(gah-zyeh-tah)
газета

(pahch-toh-vee) *(yahsh-chik)*
почтовый ящик

(chyor-nee)
чёрный

(chahsh-kah)
чашка

(poach-tah)
почта

(see-nee)
синий

(veel-kah)
вилка

(zyel-yoh-nee)
зелёный

(nohzh)
нож

(kar-tee-nah)
картина

(gah-loo-boy)
голубой

(sahl-fyet-kah)
салфетка

(dohm)
дом

(tar-yel-kah)
тарелка

(kah-bee-nyet)
кабинет

(lohzh-kah)
ложка

(shkahf)
шкаф

(koohk-nyah)
кухня

(spah-koy-nay) *(noh-chee)*
спокойной ночи

(chy)
чай

(kahk) *(dee-lah)*
Как дела?

(koh-fyeh)
кофе

(stah-loh-vah-yah)
столовая

(hah-lah-deel-neek)
холодильник

(hlyeb)
хлеб

(gah-stee-nah-yah)
гостиная

(plee-tah)
плита

(pah-zhahl-oos-tah)
пожалуйста

(gah-rahzh)
гараж

(vee-noh)
вино

(spah-see-bah)
спасибо

(pee-vah)
пиво

(eez-vee-neet-yeh)
извините

STICKY LABELS

This book has over 150 special sticky labels for you to use as you learn new words. When you are introduced to one of these words, remove the corresponding label from these pages. Be sure to use each of these unique self-adhesive labels by adhering them to a picture, window, lamp, or whatever object it refers to. And yes, they are removable! The sticky labels make learning to speak Russian much more fun and a lot easier than you ever expected. For example, when you look in the mirror and see the label, say

(zyair-kah-lah)
"зеркало."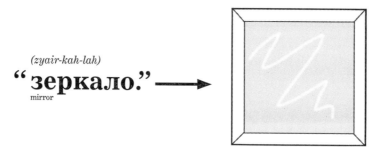
mirror

Don't just say it once, say it again and again. And once you label the refrigerator, you should never again open that door without saying

(hah-lah-deel-neek)
"холодильник."
refrigerator

By using the sticky labels, you not only learn new words, but friends and family learn along with you! The sooner you start, the sooner you can use these labels at home or work.

(dyen-gee)
Деньги
money

Before starting this Step, go back and review Step 5. It is important that you can count to

(dvahd-tset)
двадцать without looking **в** **книгу.** Let's learn the larger **числа** now. After practicing
twenty *(vuh) (kuh-nee-goo)* *(chee-slah)*
at the book numbers

(roos-skee-yeh) *(chee-slah)*
aloud **русские** numbers 10 through 11,000 below, write these **числа** in the blanks provided.
Russian

Again, notice the similarities (underlined) between **числами** such as **три** (3), **тринадцать** (13),
(chee-slah-mee) *(tree)* *(tree-nahd-tset)*
numbers

(treed-tset) *(tree-stah)* *(tih-syah-chee)*
тридцать (30), **триста** (300), and **три тысячи** (3000).

10	**десять** *(dyes-yet)*	Десять, Десять, Десять,
20	**двадцать** *(dvahd-tset)*	Двадцать, Двадцать
30	**тридцать** *(treed-tset)*	Тридцать, Тридцеть
40	**сорок** *(so-rahk)*	сорок, сорок
50	**пятьдесят** *(peed-dyes-yaht)*	Пять десят, Пятьдесят
60	**шестьдесят** *(shest-dyes-yaht)*	Шестьдесят, Шестдесят
70	**семьдесят** *(syem-dyes-yet)*	
80	**восемьдесят** *(voh-syem-dyes-yet)*	
90	**девяносто** *(dyev-yah-noh-stah)*	
100	**сто/сот/ста** *(stoh) (soht) (stah)*	
500	**пятьсот** *(pyet-soht)*	
1000	**тысяча** *(tih-syah-chah)*	

1000	**тысяча** *(tih-syah-chah)*	
2000	**две тысячи** *(tih-syah-chee)*	
3000	**три тысячи** *(tih-syah-chee)*	
4000	**четыре тысячи**	
5000	**пять тысяч** *(pyaht) (tih-syahch)*	
6000	**шесть тысяч**	
7000	**семь тысяч**	
8000	**восемь тысяч**	
9000	**девять тысяч**	
10,000	**десять тысяч**	
10,500	**десять тысяч пятьсот** *(pyet-soht)*	
11,000	**одиннадцать тысяч** *(ah-deen-nud-tset)*	

Вот две important phrases to go with all these **числа.** Say them out loud over and over and

then write them out twice as many times.

(oo) (men-yah) (yest)
у меня есть у меня есть, у меня есть, у меня есть
I have

(oo) (nahs) (yest)
у нас есть
we have

❑ **бал** *(bahl)*	ball (dance)	
❑ **балалайка** *(bah-lah-lie-kah)*	balalaika	
❑ **балерина** *(bah-leh-ree-nah)*	ballerina	**б**
❑ **балет** *(bahl-yet)*	ballet	
❑ **балкон** *(bahl-kohn)*	balcony	

The unit of currency **в** *(vuh)* in **России** *(rahs-see-ee)* Russia is the **рубль**, *(roo-bil)* abbreviated **руб.** or **р.** Let's learn the various kinds of **рублей**. *(roo-blay)* Always be sure to practice each **слово** *(sloh-vah)* out loud. You may not be able to exchange money before your arrival **в** *(vuh)* in **Россию** *(rahs-see-yoo)* so take a few minutes now to familiarize yourself with Russian and Central Asian currency.

в России

сто рублей *(stoh) (roo-blay)*

двести рублей *(dveh-stee)*

пятьсот рублей *(pyet-soht)*

тысяча рублей *(tih-syah-chah)*

пять тысяч рублей *(tih-syahch)*

десять тысяч рублей

сто тысяч рублей

в Кыргызской республике
(kir-geez-skoy) *(rehs-poo-bleek-yeh)*

в Казахстане
(kah-zahk-stahn-yeh)

в Узбекистане
(ooz-bek-ee-stahn-yeh)

❑ **банан** *(bah-nahn)*	banana		_____
❑ **бандит** *(bahn-deet)*	bandit, robber		_____
❑ **бар** *(bar)*	bar (restaurant)	**б**	_____
❑ **баржа** *(bar-zhah)*	barge		_____
❑ **барьер** *(bar-yair)*	barrier		_____

Review **числа** *(chee-slah)* **десять** *(dyes-yet)* through **десять тысяч** *(tih-syahch)* again. **Теперь,** *(tyep-yair)* **как** *(kahk)* do you say "twenty-two"
the numbers   ten   now   how

или *(ee-lee)* "fifty-three" **по-русски** *(pah-roos-skee)*? Put the numbers together in a logical sequence just as you do
or

in English. See if you can say **и** *(ee)* write out **числа** *(chee-slah)* on this **странице.** *(strah-neet-seh)* **Ответы** *(aht-vyet-ih)* are at the bottom
and   the numbers   page   answers

of **страницы.** *(strah-neet-sih)*
page

1. _____ 2. _____
(2500 = 2000 + 500)   (8350 = 8000 + 300 + 50)

3. _____ 4. _____
(4770 = 4000 + 700 + 70)   (9610 = 9000 + 600 + 10)

Now, **как** would you say the following **по-русски?**

5. _____
(I have 4000 rubles.)

6. _____
(We have 1050 rubles.)

To ask how much something costs **по-русски** *(pah-roos-skee)*, one asks — <u>**Сколько** *(skohl-kah)* **это** *(et-tah)* **стоит?** *(stoy-eet)*</u>

Now you try it. _____
(How much does that cost?)

Answer the following questions based on the numbers in parentheses.

7. **Сколько** *(skohl-kah)* **это** *(et-tah)* **стоит?** *(stoy-eet)* **Это** *(et-tah)* **стоит** *(stoy-eet)* _____ **рублей.** *(roo-blay)*
how much this   costs   this   costs   (1000)   rubles

8. **Сколько это стоит? Это стоит** _____ **рублей.** *(roo-blay)*
(5000)

9. **Сколько стоит** *(stoy-eet)* **книга** *(kuh-nee-gah)*? **Книга** *(kuh-nee-gah)* **стоит** _____ **рублей.** *(roo-blay)*
costs   the book   (6000)

10. **Сколько стоит карта** *(kar-tah)*? **Карта стоит** _____ **рублей.**
the map   (17,000)

21

8

(see-vohd-nyah) *(zahv-trah)* *(ee)* *(vchee-rah)*
Сегодня, завтра и вчера
today   tomorrow   and   yesterday

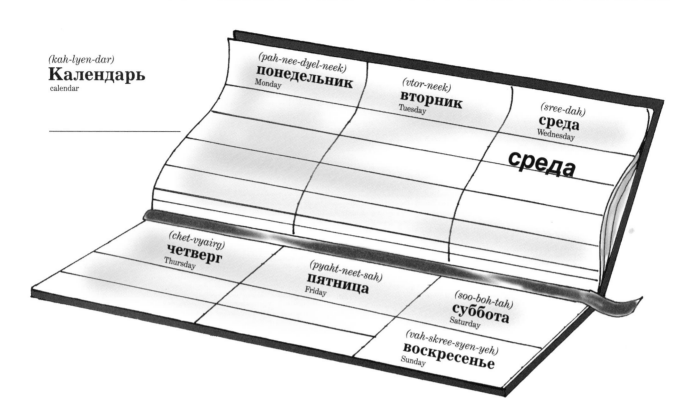

(kah-lyen-dar)
Календарь
calendar

(pah-nee-dyel-neek)
понедельник
Monday

(vtor-neek)
вторник
Tuesday

(sree-dah)
среда
Wednesday

среда

(chet-vyairg)
четверг
Thursday

(pyaht-neet-sah)
пятница
Friday

(soo-boh-tah)
суббота
Saturday

(vah-skree-syen-yeh)
воскресенье
Sunday

Learn the days of the week by writing them in the *(kah-lyen-dar-eh)* **календаре** above and then move on to the

(cheh-tir-ee) *(dyen)*
четыре parts to each **дня.**
four   day

(oo-trah)
утро
morning

(dyen)
день
day, afternoon

(vyeh-cher)
вечер
evening

(nohch)
ночь
night

❑ **бас** *(bahs)* . . . . bass (voice)
❑ **баскетбол** *(bah-sket-bohl)* . . . . basketball
❑ **батальон** *(bah-tahl-yohn)* . . . . battalion
❑ **батарея** *(bah-tar-yeh-yah)* . . . . battery
❑ **Бельгия** *(byel-gee-yah)* . . . . Belgium

б

It is *(oh-chen)* **очень** *(vahzh-nah)* **важно** to know the days of the week *(ee)* **и** the various parts of the day as well as
very *important*

these **три слова.**

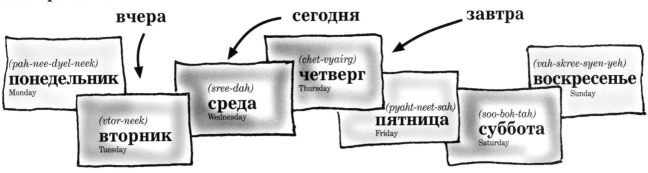

вчера   сегодня   завтра

(pah-nee-dyel-neek)
понедельник
Monday

(vtor-neek)
вторник
Tuesday

(sree-dah)
среда
Wednesday

(chet-vyairg)
четверг
Thursday

(pyaht-neet-sah)
пятница
Friday

(soo-boh-tah)
суббота
Saturday

(vah-skree-syen-yeh)
воскресенье
Sunday

(shtoh) *(see-vohd-nyah)*
Что сегодня? ———————————   *(zahv-trah)* **Что завтра?** ———————————
what (is)

(bih-lah)(vchee-rah)
Что было вчера? ———————————   *(sree-dah)* *(dah)* **Сегодня среда, да?** So ———————————
was   *yes*   *(tomorrow)*

(chet-vyairg)   *(vtor-neek)*   *(vuh)*   *(vah-skree-syen-yeh)* *(oo-trahm)*
четверг и ——————————— **вторник.** "В" can mean "on," so "в воскресенье утром"
           (yesterday)

means "on Sunday morning." Fill in the following blanks **и** then check your answers at the

(strah-neet-sih)
bottom of **страницы.**

a.   on Sunday morning   =   *в воскресенье утром* / ———————————

b.   on Friday morning   =   *в пятницу утром* / ———————————

c.   on Saturday evening   =   *в субботу вечером* / ———————————

d.   on Thursday afternoon   =   *в четверг днём* / ———————————

e.   on Thursday evening   =   *в четверг вечером* / ———————————

f.   yesterday evening   =   ———————————

g.   yesterday morning   =   ———————————

h.   tomorrow morning   =   ———————————

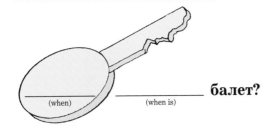

———— **балет?**
(when)   *(when is)*

———— **это?**
(who)   *(who is)*

ing the parts of **дня** *(den-yah)* / day will help you to learn the various **русские** *(roos-skee-yeh)* / Russian greetings below. Practice these every day until your trip.

(doh-brah-yeh) (oo-trah)
доброе   утро _____
good morning

(doh-brih)   (dyen)
добрый день _____
good day, hello

(doh-brih)   (vyeh-cher)
добрый вечер _____
good evening

(spah-koy-nay)   (noh-chee)
спокойной ночи _____
good night

Take the next **четыре** *(cheh-tir-ee)* / four labels **и** stick them on the appropriate things in your **доме.** *(doh-myeh)* / house Make sure you attach them to the correct items, as they are only **по-русски.** How about the bathroom mirror for **доброе   утро** *(doh-brah-yeh) (oo-trah)*"? **Или** *(ee-lee)* / or your alarm clock for "**спокойной   ночи** *(spah-koy-nay) (noh-chee)*"? Let's not forget,

(kahk)   (dee-lah)
Как дела? _____
how are you, how are things

Now for some "**да** *(dah)* / yes" or "**нет** *(nyet)* / no" questions –

Are your eyes **синие?** _____   Are your shoes **коричевые?** _____

Is your favorite color **красный?** _____   Is today **суббота?** _____

Do you own a **собака?** _____   Do you own a **кошка?** _____

You are about one-fourth of your way through **этой** *(et-toy)* / this **книги** *(kuh-nee-gee)* / book **и** it is a good time to quickly review **слова** you have learned before doing the crossword puzzle on the next **странице.** *(strah-neet-seh)* / page

(oo-dah-chee)
Удачи! Or, as one says **по-английски,** *(pah-ahn-glee-skee)* / in English "good luck to you!"
good luck

ОТВЕТЫ TO THE CROSSWORD PUZZLE

DOWN

26. окно	13. синий
25. цвет	12. дверь
24. ноль	11. пятьдесят
23. хочу	10. шестнадцать
22. пять	9. сегодня
21. красный	8. или
20. один	7. сорок
19. почта	6. кто
18. как	5. телефон
17. суп	4. туалет
16. сколько	3. коричневый
15. автомобиль	2. такси
14. балет	1. когда

ACROSS

27. это	14. оранжевый
26. стол	13. где
25. салат	12. кабинет
24. слова	11. русский
23. утро	10. нет
22. картина	9. два or две
21. кофе	8. зелёный
20. лампа	7. столовая
19. четырнадцать	6. кухня
18. открытка	5. страница
17. почему	4. да
16. стоит	3. купить
15. пятьсот	2. гостиница
	1. банк

CROSSWORD PUZZLE

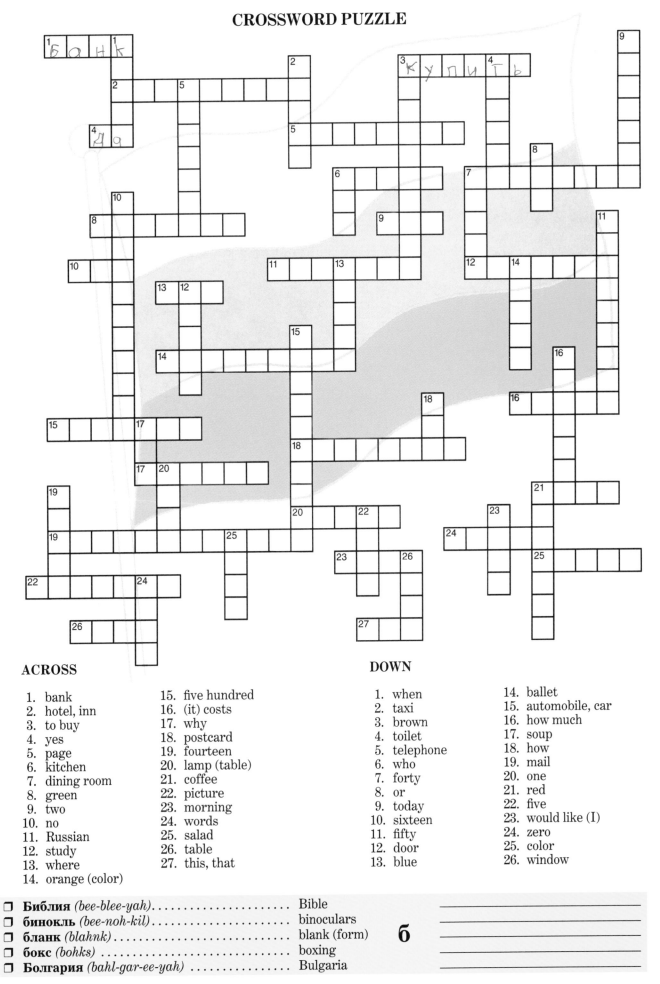

ACROSS

1. bank
2. hotel, inn
3. to buy
4. yes
5. page
6. kitchen
7. dining room
8. green
9. two
10. no
11. Russian
12. study
13. where
14. orange (color)
15. five hundred
16. (it) costs
17. why
18. postcard
19. fourteen
20. lamp (table)
21. coffee
22. picture
23. morning
24. words
25. salad
26. table
27. this, that

DOWN

1. when
2. taxi
3. brown
4. toilet
5. telephone
6. who
7. forty
8. or
9. today
10. sixteen
11. fifty
12. door
13. blue
14. ballet
15. automobile, car
16. how much
17. soup
18. how
19. mail
20. one
21. red
22. five
23. would like (I)
24. zero
25. color
26. window

б

(vuh) *(nah)* *(pohd)*
В, на, под . . .
in   on   under

(roos-skee-yeh)
Русские prepositions (words like "in," "on," "through" and "next to") are easy to learn, **и** *(ee)*
Russian

(suh) *(shest)*
they allow you to be precise **с** a minimum of effort. Instead of having to point **шесть** times
with   six

at a piece of yummy pastry you would like, you can explain precisely which one you want by

(ee-lee)
saying it is behind, in front of, next to **или** under the piece of pastry that the salesperson is

(mah-lyen-kee-ee)
starting to pick up. Let's learn some of these **маленькие слова.**
little   words

(pohd)
под _____
under

(nahd)
над _____
over

(myezh-doo)
между _____
between

(ryah-dahm) *(suh)*
рядом с _____
next to

(vuh)
в _____
into, in

(nah)
на _____
on, into

(pyeh-red)
перед _____
in front of

(zah)
за _____
behind

(eez)
из _____
out of, from

(pee-rohg)
пирог _____
cake, pie, pastry!

(strah-neet-seh)
Fill in the blanks on the next **странице** with the correct prepositions according to those you
page

just learned.

(dee-lah)
_____ _____ **дела?**
(how)   (how)   are you

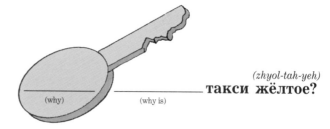

(zhyol-tah-yeh)
_____ _____ **такси жёлтое?**
(why)   (why is)

❏ **Боливия** *(bah-lee-vee-yah)*	Bolivia
❏ **бомба** *(bohm-bah)*	bomb
❏ **борщ** *(borshch)*	borsch (beet soup)
❏ **бронза** *(brohn-zah)*	bronze
❏ **брюнет** *(broo-nyet)*	brunette (male)

б _____
_____
_____
_____

(pee-rohg)
Пирог_____ **столе.**
(on) · table

(stah-lyeh)

(sah-bah-kah)
Собака_____ **столом.**
dog · (under) · table

(stah-lohm)

(vrahch)
Врач_____ **гостинице.**
doctor · (in)

(gah-stee-neet-seh)

(gdyeh) *(vrahch)*
Где врач?_____
doctor

(moozh-chee-nah)
Мужчина_____ **гостиницей.**
man · (in front of) · hotel

(gah-stee-neet-say)

(moozh-chee-nah)
Где мужчина?_____
man

(teh-leh-fohn)
Телефон_____ **картиной.**
telephone · (next to) · picture

(kar-tee-noy)

(teh-leh-fohn)
Где телефон?_____
telephone

(tyep-yair)
Теперь fill in each blank on the picture below with the best possible one of these **маленькие**
now · little *(mah-lyen-kee-ee)*

слова. Do you recognize the towers of **Собора Василия Блаженного?**
words · *(sah-boh-rah)* *(vah-see-lee-yah)* *(blah-zhen-nah-vah)*

_____
(over)

_____
(behind)

_____
(on)

_____
(next to)

_____
(between)

_____
(in)

_____
(in front of)

_____
(under)

(vuh) *(yahn-var-yeh)* *(fyev-rahl-yeh)* *(mart-yeh)*

В январе, феврале, марте

in   January   February   March

You have learned *(dnee)* *(nee-dyel-ee)* **дни недели,** so now it is time to learn *(myes-yet-sih)* *(go-dah)* **месяцы года и** all the different
days (of) week   months (of)   year

kinds of *(pah-go-dih)* **погоды.**
weather

Январь

Февраль

Март

Апрель

Май

Июнь

Июль

Август

Сентябрь

Октябрь

Ноябрь

Декабрь

When someone asks, " *(kah-kah-yah)* *(see-vohd-nyah)* *(pah-go-dah)* **Какая сегодня погода?**" you have a variety of answers. Let's
    how is   today   weather

learn them but first, does this sound familiar?

(treed-tset)	*(dnay)*		*(syen-tyah-bryeh)*	*(ahp-ryel-yeh)*	*(ee-yoon-yeh)*		*(nah-yah-bryeh)*
Тридцать	**дней**	**в**	**сентябре,**	**апреле,**	**июне**	**и**	**ноябре.**
thirty	days		September	April	June		November

❑ **веранда** *(vee-rahn-dah)*	veranda		
❑ **витамин** *(vee-tah-meen)*	vitamin		
❑ **водка** *(vohd-kah)*	vodka	**в**	
❑ **Волга** *(vohl-gah)*	Volga River		
❑ **волейбол** *(vah-lay-bohl)*	volleyball		

(kah-kah-yah) (see-vohd-nyah) (pah-go-dah)
Какая   сегодня   погода? _____

(vuh)(yahn-var-yeh) (ee-dyoht)(snyeg)
В январе   идёт снег. _____
in   January   it snows

(fyev-rahl-yeh)
В феврале идёт снег. _____
February   it snows

(mart-yeh)   (dohzhd)
В марте идёт дождь. _____
                it rains

(ahp-ryel-yeh)   (dohzhd)
В апреле идёт дождь. _____

(mah-yeh) (vyet-ren-ah)
В мае   ветрено. _____
          windy

(ee-yoon-yeh) (vyet-ren-ah)
В июне   ветрено. _____
June

(ee-yool-yeh) (zhar-kah)
В июле   жарко. _____
          hot

(ahv-goost-yeh)
В августе   жарко. _____
              hot

(syen-tyah-bryeh) (hah-roh-shah-yah) (pah-go-dah)
В сентябре   хорошая   погода. _____
September   good   weather

(ahk-tyah-bryeh) (hoh-lahd-nah)
В октябре   холодно. _____
              cold

(nah-yah-bryeh) (hoh-lahd-nah)
В ноябре   холодно. _____
              cold

(dee-kah-bryeh) (plah-hah-yah)
В декабре   плохая   погода. _____
              bad

(kah-kah-yah) (pah-go-dah) (vuh) (fyev-rahl-yeh)
Какая   погода   в   феврале? _____
how is   February

(ahp-ryel-yeh)
Какая погода в апреле? _____
                April

(nah-yah-bryeh)
Какая погода в ноябре? _____
                November

(ahv-goost-yeh)
Какая погода в августе? _____
                August

❐ **газ** *(gahz)* . . . . natural gas
❐ **газета** *(gah-zyeh-tah)* . . . . gazette, newspaper
❐ **— газетчик** *(gah-zyet-cheek)* . . . . newspaper man **Г**
❐ **галерея** *(gahl-yair-eh-yah)* . . . . gallery
❐ **генерал** *(gee-nee-rahl)* . . . . general

Теперь for the seasons of **года** . . .
year

(zee-moy)
зимой
in winter

(lyet-ahm)
летом
in summer

(oh-syen-yoo)
осенью
in autumn

(vees-noy)
весной
in spring

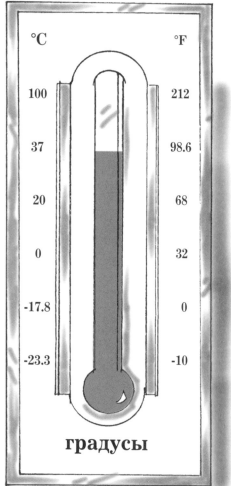

(tsel-see)
Цельсий
Celsius

(fah-ren-gate)
Фаренгейт
Fahrenheit

°C   **°F**

°C	°F
100	212
37	98.6
20	68
0	32
-17.8	0
-23.3	-10

градусы

At this point, it is **хорошая** *(hah-roh-shah-yah)* idea to familiarize
good
yourself **с** *(suh)* **русскими** *(roos-skee-mee)* **температурами.** *(tem-pee-rah-too-rah-mee)*
temperatures

Carefully study the thermometer because

(tem-pee-rah-too-rih)
температуры в России are calculated on the

basis of Celsius (not Fahrenheit).

To convert °C to °F, multiply by 1.8 and add 32.

37 °C x 1.8 = 66.6 + 32 = 98.6 °F

To convert °F to °C, subtract 32 and multiply by
0.55.

98.6 °F - 32 = 66.6 x 0.55 = 37 °C

(kah-kah-yah)   *(nar-mahl-nah-yah)*   *(tsel-see-yoo)*
Какая температура нормальная по Цельсию?
normal   Celsius

(zah-myair-zah-nee-yah)
Какая температура замерзания по Цельсию?
freezing point

☐ **Греция** *(gret-see-yah)* . . . . Greece
☐ — where they speak **по-гречески** *(pah-greh-chee-skee)*
☐ **география** *(gee-ah-grah-fee-yah)* . . . . geography
☐ **геология** *(gee-ah-loh-gee-yah)* . . . . geology
☐ — **геолог** *(gee-oh-lahg)* . . . . geologist

Г

11

Семья и дом
(syem-yah) (dohm)
family house

One of the charming aspects **в** *(vuh)* **России** concerns names. A father's first name becomes the middle name for both his sons **и** daughters. Daughters add **-овна** *(ohv-nah)*, **-евна** *(yev-nah)*, or **-ична** *(eech-nah)* to the father's first name **а** *(ah)* and sons add **-ович** *(ah-veech)*, **-евич** *(yev-eech)*, or **-ич** *(eech)*. Both the individual's first name **и** the father's name (patronymic) are constantly used **по-русски** *(pah-roos-skee)*. Study the family tree below **и** then practice these new words on the next **странице**.

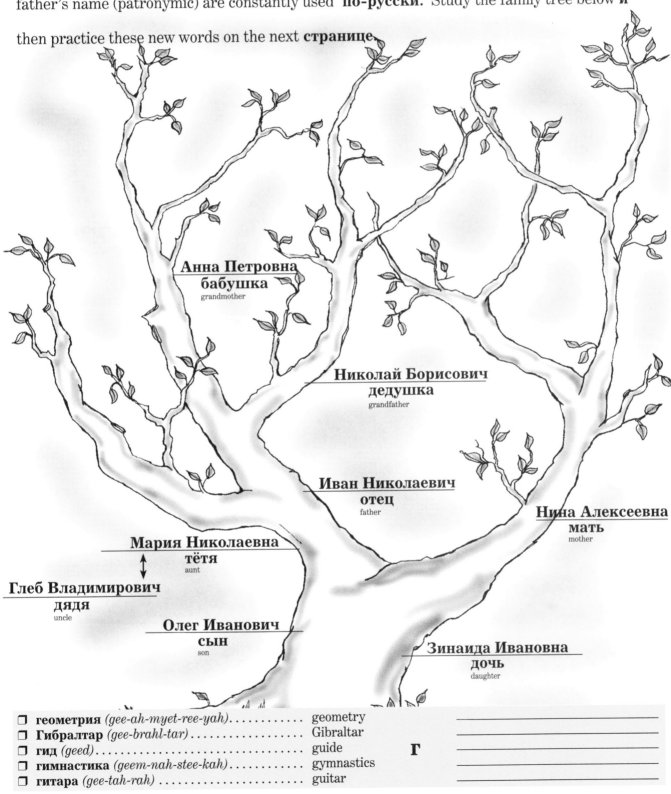

Анна Петровна
бабушка
grandmother

Николай Борисович
дедушка
grandfather

Иван Николаевич
отец
father

Нина Алексеевна
мать
mother

Мария Николаевна
тётя
aunt

Глеб Владимирович
дядя
uncle

Олег Иванович
сын
son

Зинаида Ивановна
дочь
daughter

❏ **геометрия** *(gee-ah-myet-ree-yah)*	geometry	
❏ **Гибралтар** *(gee-brahl-tar)*	Gibraltar	
❏ **гид** *(geed)*	guide	**Г**
❏ **гимнастика** *(geem-nah-stee-kah)*	gymnastics	
❏ **гитара** *(gee-tah-rah)*	guitar	

Let's learn how to identify *(syem-yah)* **"семья"** by name. Study the following examples carefully.
family

(vahs) *(zah-voot)*
Как вас зовут?_____
how are you called

(men-yah) *(zah-voot)*
Меня зовут_____
I am called   (your name)

(rah-dee-tee-lee)
родители
parents

(aht-yets)
отец_____
father

(kahk) *(zah-voot)* *(aht-tsah)* *(aht-tsah)* *(zah-voot)*
Как зовут отца? Отца зовут *Иван* .
how is called father father is called

(maht)
мать_____
mother

(kahk) *(zah-voot)* *(maht)* *(maht)* *(zah-voot)*
Как зовут мать? Мать зовут_____.
how is called mother mother is called

(dyeh-tee)
дети
children

(sin) *(dohch)* *(braht)* *(see-strah)*
Сын и дочь = брат и сестра!
brother sister

(sin)
сын _____
son

(kahk) *(zah-voot)* *(sin-ah)*
Как зовут сына? Сына зовут_____.
how is called son

(dohch)
дочь_____
daughter

(kahk) *(zah-voot)* *(dohch)*
Как зовут дочь? Дочь зовут_____.
daughter

(rohd-stveen-nee-kee)
родственники
relatives

(dyeh-doosh-kah)
дедушка _____
grandfather

(zah-voot) *(dyeh-doosh-koo)*
Как зовут дедушку?_____
how is called grandfather

(bah-boosh-kah)
бабушка _____
grandmother

(bah-boosh-koo)
Как зовут бабушку?_____
grandmother

Now you ask —

_____
(how are you called, what's your name?)

And answer —

_____
(my name is . . .)

❑ **грамм** *(grahm)*	. . . .	gram		_____
❑ **гранит** *(grah-neet)*	. . . .	granite		_____
❑ **группа** *(groop-pah)*	. . . .	group	**Г**	_____
❑ **ГУМ** *(goom)*	. . . .	department store in Moscow		_____
❑ **гусь** *(goose)*	. . . .	goose		_____

(koohk-nyah)

Кухня
kitchen

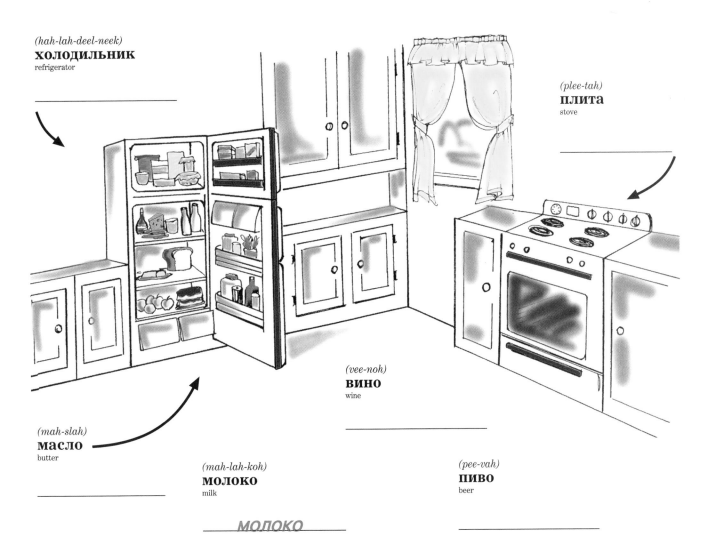

(hah-lah-deel-neek)
холодильник
refrigerator

_____

(plee-tah)
плита
stove

_____

(vee-noh)
вино
wine

_____

(mah-slah)
масло
butter

_____

(mah-lah-koh)
МОЛОКО
milk

МОЛОКО _____

(pee-vah)
ПИВО
beer

_____

Answer these *(vah-proh-sih)* **вопросы** aloud.
questions

(gdyeh) *(pee-vah)*
Где пиво? . . . . **Пиво в холодильнике.** *(vuh) (hah-lah-deel-neek-yeh)*
beer   refrigerator

(mah-lah-koh)   *(vee-noh)*   *(bah-nahn)*   *(sah-laht)*   *(mah-slah)*
Где молоко?   **Где вино?**   **Где банан?**   **Где салат?**   **Где масло?**
milk   wine   salad   butter

Теперь open your **книгу** *(kuh-nee-goo)* **на** *(nah)* **странице** *(strah-neet-seh)* **с** *(suh)* the labels **и** remove the next group of labels **и**
book   to

proceed to label all these things in your **кухне.** *(kookh-nyeh)*
kitchen

❏ **дама** *(dah-mah)*	dame, lady, woman	_____
❏ **Дания** *(dah-nee-yah)*	Denmark	_____
❏ — where they speak **по-датски** *(pah-daht-skee)*	**Д**	_____
❏ **дата** *(dah-tah)*	date	_____
❏ **делегат** *(dyeh-leh-gaht)*	delegate	_____

33

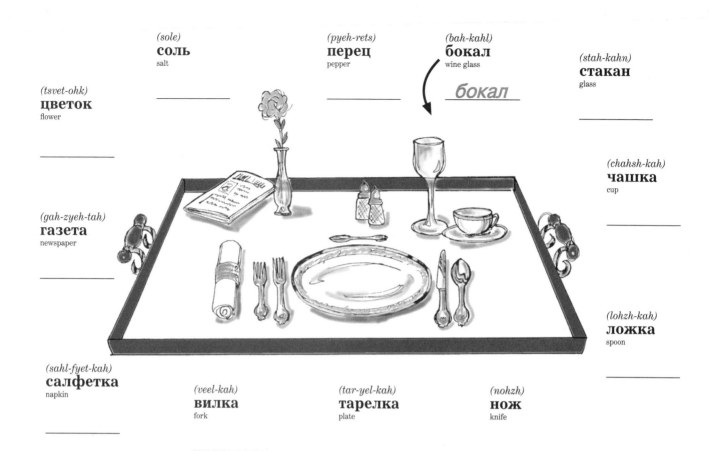

(sole)
соль
salt

(pyeh-rets)
перец
pepper

(bah-kahl)
бокал
wine glass

бокал

(stah-kahn)
стакан
glass

(tsvet-ohk)
цветок
flower

_____

_____

(gah-zyeh-tah)
газета
newspaper

_____

(chahsh-kah)
чашка
cup

_____

(lohzh-kah)
ложка
spoon

(sahl-fyet-kah)
салфетка
napkin

_____

(veel-kah)
вилка
fork

_____

(tar-yel-kah)
тарелка
plate

_____

(nohzh)
нож
knife

_____

И more . . .

(shkahf)
шкаф_____
cupboard

(chy)
чай_____
tea

(chy)
Где чай?
tea

(shkah-foo)
Чай в шкафу.

(koh-fyeh)
кофе_____
coffee

(koh-fyeh)
Где кофе?_____
coffee

(hlyeb)
хлеб_____
bread

(gdyeh)
Где хлеб?_____
bread

Don't forget to label all these things and do not forget to use every opportunity to say these **слова** out loud. **Это очень важно.**

(oh-chen) very *(vahzh-nah)* important

❏ **демонстрация** *(dyeh-mahn-straht-see-yah)* .. demonstration _____
❏ **джаз** *(dzhahz)*.......................... jazz _____
❏ **джин** *(dzheen)* .... gin **Д** _____
❏ **диагноз** *(dee-ahg-nahz)* .... diagnosis _____
❏ **диаграмма** *(dee-ah-grahm-mah)* .... diagram, blueprint _____

(krah-vaht) **кровать**	*(aht-krit-kah)* **открытка**	*(rahs-chohs-kah)* **расчёска**	*(shohr-tih)* **шорты**
(pah-doosh-kah) **подушка**	*(pahs-part)* **паспорт**	*(pahl-toh)* **пальто**	*(my-kah)* **майка**
(ah-dee-yah-lah) **одеяло**	*(beel-yet)* **билет**	*(zohn-teek)* **зонтик**	*(troo-sih)* **трусы**
(boo-deel-neek) **будильник**	*(cheh-mah-dahn)* **чемодан**	*(plahshch)* **плащ**	*(my-kah)* **майка**
	(soom-kah) **сумка**	*(pyair-chaht-kee)* **перчатки**	*(plaht-yeh)* **платье**
(oo-mih-vahl-neek) **умывальник**	*(boo-mahzh-neek)* **бумажник**	*(shlyah-pah)* **шляпа**	*(blooz-kah)* **блузка**
(pah-lah-tyent-sah) **полотенца**	*(dyen-gee)* **деньги**	*(shlyah-pah)* **шляпа**	*(yoob-kah)* **юбка**
(too-ahl-yet) **туалет**	*(kreh-deet-nah-yah)* *(kar-tahch-kah)* **кредитная карточка**	*(sah-pah-gee)* **сапоги**	*(svee-tyair)* **свитер**
(doosh) **душ**	*(dah-rohzh-nih-yeh)* *(cheh-kee)* **дорожные чеки**	*(too-flee)* **туфли**	*(kahm-bee-naht-see-yah)* **комбинация**
(kah-rahn-dahsh) **карандаш**	*(foh-tah-ahp-pah-raht)* **фотоаппарат**	*(krahs-sohv-kee)* **кроссовке**	*(leef-cheek)* **лифчик**
(teh-leh-vee-zar) **телевизор**	*(foh-tah-plyohn-kah)* **фотоплёнка**	*(kahst-yoom)* **костюм**	*(troo-sih)* **трусы**
(rooch-kah) **ручка**	*(koo-pahl-nee)* *(kahst-yoom)* **купальный костюм**	*(gahl-stook)* **галстук**	*(nah-skee)* **носки**
(zhoor-nahl) **журнал**	*(koo-pahl-nee)* *(kahst-yoom)* **купальный костюм**	*(roo-bahsh-kah)* **рубашка**	*(kahl-goht-kee)* **колготки**
(kuh-nee-gah) **книга**	*(sahn-dahl-ee-ee)* **сандалии**	*(plah-tohk)* **платок**	*(pee-zhah-mah)* **пижама**
(kahmp-yoo-tyer) **компьютер**	*(tyohm-nih-yeh)* *(ahch-kee)* **тёмные очки**	*(peed-zhahk)* **пиджак**	*(nahch-nah-yah)* *(roo-bahsh-kah)* **ночная рубашка**
(ahch-kee) **очки**	*(zoob-nah-yah)* *(shchoht-kah)* **зубная щётка**	*(bryoo-kee)* **брюки**	*(bahn-nee)* *(hah-laht)* **банный халат**
(boo-mah-gah) **бумага**	*(zoob-nah-yah)* *(pahs-tah)* **зубная паста**	*(dzheen-sih)* **джинсы**	*(tah-poach-kee)* **тапочки**
(kar-zee-nah) **корзина**	*(mwee-lah)* **мыло**	*(yah)* *(ah-myeh-ree-kah-nyets)* **Я американец.**	
(pees-moh) **письмо**	*(breet-vah)* **бритва**	*(yah)* *(hah-choo)* *(ee-zoo-chaht)* *(roos-skee)* **Я хочу изучать русский.**	
(mar-kah) **марка**	*(dyeh-zah-dah-rahnt)* **дезодорант**	*(men-yah)* *(zah-voot)* **Меня зовут _____ .**	

PLUS...

This book includes a number of other innovative features unique to the **"10 minutes a day®"** Series. At the back of this book, you will find twelve pages of flash cards. Cut them out and flip through them at least once a day.

On pages 116, 117 and 118 you will find a beverage guide and a menu guide. Don't wait until your trip to use them. Clip out the menu guide and use it tonight at the dinner table. Take them both with you the next time you dine at your favorite Russian restaurant.

By using the special features in this book, you will be speaking Russian before you know it.

(oo-dah-chee)
Удачи!
good luck

(ree-lee-gee-ee)
Религии
religions

(vuh)   *(ree-lee-gee-ee)*
В   **России** there is a wide variety of **религий.**
religions

(ree-lee-gee-yah)
A person's **религия** is usually one of the following.
religion

(prah-vah-slahv-nah-yah)
1. **православная** _____
   Orthodox woman

(prah-vah-slahv-nee)
   православный _____
   Orthodox man

(yev-ray-kah)
2. **еврейка** _____
   Jewish woman

(yev-ray)
   еврей *еврей, еврей, еврей*
   Jewish man

(kah-tah-leech-kah)
3. **католичка** _____
   Catholic woman

(kah-toh-leek)
   католик _____
   Catholic man

(moo-sool-mahn-kah)
4. **мусульманка** _____
   Moslem woman

(moo-sool-mah-neen)
   мусульманин _____
   Moslem man

(mnoh-gah) (krah-see-vik) (tsair-kvay)   *(vuh)*
You will see **много красивых церквей** like this during your holiday **в**   **России. Теперь**
    many   pretty   churches

                     (pah-roos-skee)   *(yah)*
let's learn how to say "I am" **по-русски: я**   *Я, Я, Я* _____
                                    I am

Test yourself - write each sentence on the next page for more practice. Add your own personal

variations as well.

(how much) _____ **это?**
                       (how much)

❏ **диван** *(dee-vahn)*	divan, sofa		_____
❏ **дизель** *(dee-zyel)*	diesel		_____
❏ **диплом** *(dee-plohm)*	diploma	**Д**	_____
❏ **дипломат** *(dee-plah-maht)*	diplomat		_____
❏ **директор** *(dee-rek-tar)*	director		_____

(kah-tah-leech-kah)

Я католичка. _____

(prah-vah-slahv-nah-yah)

Я православная. _____

(yev-ray)

Я еврей. _____

(ah-myeh-ree-kah-nyets)

Я американец. _____
American

(vuh) (rahs-see-ee)

Я в России. _____

(kah-nah-dyets)

Я канадец. _____
Canadian

(yah) (vuh) (tsair-kvee)

Я в церкви. _____
I (am) in   church

(yah) (koohk-nyeh)

Я в кухне. _____

(moo-sool-mah-neen)

Я мусульманин. _____

(yev-ray-kah)

Я еврейка. _____

(gah-stee-neet-seh)

Я в гостинице. _____
hotel

(res-tah-rahn-yeh)

Я в ресторане. _____
restaurant

(hah-choo) (yest)

Я хочу есть. _____
want to   eat, I'm hungry

(hah-choo) (peet)

Я хочу пить. _____
want to   drink, I'm thirsty

To negate any of these statements, simply add " *(nyeh)* **не** " after "**Я.**"
not

(nyeh) (kah-tah-leech-kah)

Я не католичка. _____
I (am) not

(yev-ray)

Я не еврей. _____

Go through and drill these sentences again but with " *(nyeh)* **не.**"

Теперь take a piece of paper. Our *(syem-yah)* **семья** from earlier had a reunion. Identify everyone

below by writing *(prah-veel-nah-yeh) (roos-skah-yeh)* **правильное русское слово** for each person — *(maht)* **мать,** *(dohch)* **дочь** and so on.
correct

Don't forget the *(sah-bah-kah)* **собака!**

- □ **дискуссия** *(dee-skoos-see-yah)* .... discussion
- □ **доктор** *(dohk-tar)* .... doctor
- □ **документ** *(dah-koo-myent)* .... document   **Д**
- □ **доллар** *(dohl-lar)* .... dollar
- □ **драма** *(drah-mah)* .... drama

You have already used **два** very important verbs: *(yah)* *(hah-choo)* **я хочу** and *(oo)* *(men-yah)* *(yest)* **у меня есть.** Although
I would like   I have

you might be able to get by with only these verbs, let's assume you want to do better. First a

quick review.

How do you say   "I"   *(pah-roos-skee)* **по-русски?** _____

How do you say   "we"   **по-русски?** _____

Compare these *(dvah)* **два** charts *(oh-chen)* **очень** carefully **и** learn these *(shest)* **шесть** *(slohv)* **слов** now.
two   very   six

		(yah)				*(mwee)*	
I	=	**я**	_____	we	=	**мы**	_____
he	=	*(ohn)* **он**	_____	you	=	*(vwee)* **вы**	_____
she	=	*(ah-nah)* **она**	_____	they	=	*(ah-nee)* **они**	_____

Not too hard, is it? Draw lines between the matching English **и русские** *(roos-skee-yeh)* *(slah-vah)* **слова** below to

see if you can keep these **слова** straight in your mind.

(mwee)
мы   I

(ohn)
он   you

(ah-nee)
они   he

(yah)
я   we

(vwee)
вы   she

(ah-nah)
она   they

❑ **жакет** *(zhah-kyet)*	jacket	
❑ **жасмин** *(zhahs-meen)*	jasmine	
❑ **желе** *(zhel-yeh)*	jelly	**Ж**
❑ **журнал** *(zhoor-nahl)*	journal, magazine	
❑ **— журналист** *(zhoor-nah-leest)*	journalist	

(tyep-yair) *(ee)* *(boo-mahg-yeh)* *(vwee)*
Теперь close **книгу** **и** write out both columns of this practice on **бумаге**. How did **вы** do?
paper

(hah-rah-shoh) *(ploh-hah)* *(hah-rah-shoh)* *(nyet)* *(vwee)* *(vwee)*
Хорошо или плохо? Хорошо или нет? Теперь that **вы** know these **слова, вы** can say
good   or   bad   good   not   you   you

almost anything **по-русски** with one basic formula: the "plug-in" formula.

(shest)
To demonstrate, let's take **шесть** basic **и** practical verbs **и** see how the "plug-in" formula works.
six

Write the verbs in the blanks after **вы** have practiced saying them out loud many times.

(zah-kah-zih-vaht)
заказывать _____
to order, to reserve

(pahv-tar-yaht)
повторять _____
to repeat

(pah-koo-paht)
покупать *покупать, покупать*
to buy

(pah-nee-maht)
понимать _____
to understand

(ee-zoo-chaht)
изучать _____
to learn

(gah-vah-reet)
говорить _____
to speak

(vwee) *(cheh-tir-ee)*
Besides the familiar words already circled, can **вы** find **четыре** of the above verbs in the

puzzle below? When **вы** find them, write them in the blanks to the right.

Ю	К	О	Г	Д	А	С	Э	Ц	Ч	П
Ф	О	П	О	К	У	П	А	Т	Ь	Я
Э	Ш	Э	В	Ы	Ж	И	Г	Д	Е	Т
Ч	К	П	О	В	Т	О	Р	Я	Т	Ь
Й	А	Я	Р	К	Д	Ш	Ю	С	Р	Щ
П	О	Н	И	М	А	Т	Ь	Ё	И	Ф
О	Н	И	Т	Ц	Ы	К	Т	О	Й	Х
Х	А	З	Ь	Ж	В	Б	А	Л	Е	Т

1._____

2._____

3._____

4._____

Study the following patterns carefully.

	(zah-kah-zih-vah-yoo) **заказываю**	= I *order*
	(pah-koo-pah-yoo) **покупаю**	= I *buy*
(yah) **я**	*(ee-zoo-chah-yoo)* **изучаю**	= I *learn*
	(pahv-tar-yah-yoo) **повторяю**	= I *repeat*
	(pah-nee-mah-yoo) **понимаю**	= I *understand*
	(gah-vah-ryoo) **говорю**	= I *speak*

	(zah-kah-zih-vah-yet) **заказывает**	= he / she *orders*
	(pah-koo-pah-yet) **покупает**	= he / she *buys*
(ohn) **он**	*(ee-zoo-chah-yet)* **изучает**	= he / she *learns*
(ah-nah) **она**	*(pahv-tar-yah-yet)* **повторяет**	= he / she *repeats*
	(pah-nee-mah-yet) **понимает**	= he / she *understands*
	(gah-vah-reet) **говорит**	= he / she *speaks*

Note:
- With all these verbs, the first thing you do is drop the final **"ть"** from the basic verb form.

- With **я,** you add **-ю** *(yoo)* or **-у** *(oo)* to the basic verb form. This is basically the sound *"oo."*

- With **он** or **она,** you add the sound *"yet"* **(-ет)** to the basic verb form or the sound *"eet"* **(-ит).**

Some verbs just will not conform to the pattern! But don't worry. Speak slowly **и** clearly, **и** you will be perfectly understood whether you say **изучаю** *(ee-zoo-chah-yoo)* or **изучает.** *(ee-zoo-chah-yet)* **Русские** Russians will be delighted that you have taken the time to learn their language.

Here's your pattern for **мы.** *(mwee)* we Add the sound *"yem"* **(-ем)** or *"eem"* **(-им).**

	(zah-kah-zih-vah-yem) **заказываем**	= we *order*
мы	*(pah-koo-pah-yem)* **покупаем**	= we *buy*
	(ee-zoo-chah-yem) **изучаем**	= we *learn*

	(pahv-tar-yah-yem) **повторяем**	= we *repeat*
мы	*(pah-nee-mah-yem)* **понимаем**	= we *understand*
	(gah-vah-reem) **говорим**	= we *speak*

❏ **инженер** *(een-zhyen-yair)*	. . . .	engineer
❏ **инспектор** *(een-spyek-tar)*	. . . .	inspector
❏ **институт** *(een-stee-toot)*	. . . .	institute
❏ **инструктор** *(een-strook-tar)*	. . . .	instructor
❏ **инструмент** *(een-stroo-myent)*	. . . .	instrument

И

_____
_____
_____
_____
_____

Here's your pattern for **вы** *(vwee)*. Add the sound "*yet-yeh*" **(-ете)** or "*eet-yeh*" **(-ите)**.

	(zah-kah-zih-vah-yet-yeh) **заказываете**	=	you *order*
вы	*(pah-koo-pah-yet-yeh)* **покупаете**	=	you *buy*
	(ee-zoo-chah-yet-yeh) **изучаете**	=	you *learn*

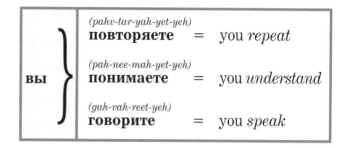

	(pahv-tar-yah-yet-yeh) **повторяете**	=	you *repeat*
вы	*(pah-nee-mah-yet-yeh)* **понимаете**	=	you *understand*
	(gah-vah-reet-yeh) **говорите**	=	you *speak*

Here's your pattern for **они,** *(ah-nee)* *they* which calls for the sound "*yoot*" **(-ют)** or sometimes "*yaht*" **(-ят)**.

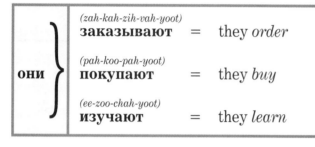

	(zah-kah-zih-vah-yoot) **заказывают**	=	they *order*
они	*(pah-koo-pah-yoot)* **покупают**	=	they *buy*
	(ee-zoo-chah-yoot) **изучают**	=	they *learn*

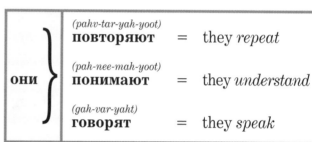

	(pahv-tar-yah-yoot) **повторяют**	=	they *repeat*
они	*(pah-nee-mah-yoot)* **понимают**	=	they *understand*
	(gah-var-yaht) **говорят**	=	they *speak*

Вот **шесть** more verbs.
(voht) *(shest)*
here are six

(yek-haht)
ехать _____
to go (by vehicle), to ride

(zheet)
жить _____
to live, to reside

(pree-yez-zhaht)
приезжать _____
to arrive

(zhdaht)
ждать _____
to wait for

(vee-dyet)
видеть _____
to see

(ees-kaht)
искать _____
to look for

At the back of **книги,** **вы** will find twelve *(kuh-nee-gee)*

(strah-neets)
страниц of flash cards to help you learn
pages

(noh-vih-yeh)
новые **слова.** Cut them out; carry them in
new

your briefcase, purse, pocket **или** knapsack; **и**

review them whenever **вы** *(vwee)* have a free moment.

❐ **интеллигент** *(een-tyel-lee-gyent)*	intellectual		
❐ **интервью** *(een-tyair-view)*	interview		_____
❐ **интерес** *(een-tyair-yes)*	interest	**и**	_____
❐ **интернациональный** *(een-tyair-naht-see-ah-nahl-nee)* ..	international		_____
❐ **информация** *(een-far-maht-see-yah)*	information		_____

42

Теперь it is your turn to practice *(shtoh)* **что** *(vwee)* **вы** have learned. Fill in the following blanks with the
correct form of the verb. Each time **вы** write out the sentence, be sure to say it aloud.

(zah-kah-zih-vaht)
заказывать
to order, to reserve

(yah)
Я _____ *(stah-kahn)* *(vah-dih)* **стакан воды.**
glass   water

(bah-kahl) *(vee-nah)*
Он _____ **бокал вина.**
Она

(mwee)
Мы _____ *(mah-lah-kah)* **стакан молока.**

(vwee)
Вы _____ *(chahsh-kee)* *(chah-yah)* **две чашки чая.**
cups (of)   tea

(ah-nee)
Они _____ *(koh-fyeh)* **три чашки кофе.**

(pah-koo-paht)
покупать
to buy

Я _____ **книгу.**
book

Он *покупает/* _____ **салат.**
Она

(lahm-poo)
Мы _____ **лампу.**

(chah-sih)
Вы _____ **часы.**
clock

(beel-yet)
Они _____ **билет.**
ticket

(ee-zoo-chaht)
изучать
to learn

(roos-skee)
Я _____ **русский.**
Russian

Он _____ **русский.**
Она

(ahn-glee-skee)
Мы _____ **английский.**
English

Вы *изучаете/* _____ **английский.**

(nee-myet-skee)
Они _____ **немецкий.**
German

(pahv-tar-yaht)
повторять что? что? что?
to repeat

(yah)
Я _____ *(sloh-vah)* **слово.**

(aht-vyet-ih)
Он _____ **ответы.**
Она   answers

Мы _____ **ответы.**

(chee-sloh)
Вы _____ **число.**
numbers

(vah-proh-sih)
Они _____ **вопросы.**
questions

(pah-nee-maht)
понимать
to understand

(pah-ahn-glee-skee)
Я _____ **по-английски.**

Он _____ **по-русски.**
Она

(pah-nee-myet-skee)
Мы _____ **по-немецки.**
German

(pah-frahn-tsoo-skee)
Вы _____ **по-французски.**
French

(pah-ee-spahn-skee)
Они _____ **по-испански.**
Spanish

(gah-vah-reet)
говорить Как дела?
to speak, to say

(pah-roos-skee)
Я _____ **по-русски.**
Russian

Он _____ **по-английски.**
Она

(pah-ee-tahl-yahn-skee)
Мы _____ **по-итальянски.**
Italian

Вы _____ **по-русски.**

Они _____ **по-английски.**

❏ **Исландия** *(ees-lahn-dee-yah)* . . . . Iceland
❏ **история** *(ees-toh-ree-yah)* . . . . history   **И** _____
❏ **Италия** *(ee-tah-lee-yah)* . . . . Italy   _____
❏ — where they speak **по-итальянски** *(pah-ee-tahl-yahn-skee)* **К** _____
❏ **кабина** *(kah-bee-nah)* . . . . cabin, booth _____

Now take a break, walk around the room, take a deep breath and do the next six verbs.

(yek-haht)
ехать
to go, to ride

Я _____ в Россию. *(vuh) (rahs-see-yoo)*
to

Он _едет/_____ в Москву. *(mahsk-voo)*
Она

Мы _едем/_____ в Петербург. *(pyeh-tyair-boorg)*

Вы _____ в гостиницу. *(gah-stee-neet-soo)*
hotel

Они _____ в Нижний Новгород. *(neezh-nee) (nohv-gah-rohd)*
Nizhny Novgorod

(pree-yez-zhaht)
приезжать
to arrive

Я _____ из Москвы. *(eez) (mahsk-vih)*
from

Он _____ из Канады. *(eez) (kah-nah-dih)*
Она Canada

Мы _____ из России. *(rahs-see-ee)*

Вы _____ из Петербурга. *(pyeh-tyair-boor-gah)*

Они _____ из Австралии. *(ahv-strah-lee-ee)*
Australia

(vee-dyet)
видеть
to see

Я _____ гостиницу. *(gah-stee-neet-soo)*
hotel

Он _____ такси. *(tahk-see)*
Она taxi

Мы _видим/_____ ресторан. *(res-tah-rahn)*
restaurant

Вы _____ банк. *(bahnk)*
bank

Они _____ Москву. *(mahsk-voo)*

(zheet)
жить
to live, to reside

Я _____ в России. *(vuh) (rahs-see-ee)*

Он _живёт/_____ в Америке. *(ah-myeh-ree-kyeh)*
Она America

Мы _живём/_____ в Канаде. *(kah-nah-dyeh)*
Canada
Вы _____ в Англии. *(ahn-glee-ee)*
England

Они _____ в Австралии. *(ahv-strah-lee-ee)*
Australia

(zhdaht)
ждать
to wait for

Я _____ такси. *(tahk-see)*

Он _____ автобуса. *(ahv-toh-boo-sah)*
Она bus

Мы _ждём/_____ Ивана. *(ee-vah-nah)*
Ivan

Вы _ждёте/_____ Анну. *(ahn-noo)*
Anna

Они _____ меню. *(men-yoo)*
menu

(ess-kaht)
искать
to look for

Я _____ марку. *(mar-koo)*
stamp

Он _ищет/_____ цветы. *(tsvet-ih)*
Она flowers

Мы _ищем/_____ туалет. *(too-ahl-yet)*

Вы _____ дом. *(dohm)*
house

Они _____ книгу. *(kuh-nee-goo)*
book

(dah)
Да, it is hard to get used to all those **новым словам.** But just keep practicing **и,** before **вы**
(noh-vim) *(ee)* *(vwee)*
yes   new

know it, **вы** will be using them naturally. **Теперь** is a perfect time to turn to the back of this

(kuh-nee-gee)
книги, clip out your verb flash cards **и** start flashing. Don't skip over your free **слова** either.

Check them off in the box provided as **вы изучаете** each one. See if **вы** can fill in the
(ee-zoo-chah-yet-yeh) *(vwee)*
learn

blanks below. The correct **ответы** are at the bottom of **этой страницы.**
(et-toy)
this

1. _____
(I speak Russian.)

2. _____
(We learn Russian.)

3. _____
(She understands English.)

4. _____
(He arrives from America.)

5. _____
(They live in Canada.)

6. _____
(You buy a book.)

In the following Steps, **вы** will be introduced
(vwee)

to more verbs **и вы** should drill them in

exactly the same way as **вы** did in this
(vwee)

section. Look up **новые слова** in your
(noh-vih-yeh)
new

словаре и make up your own sentences.
(slah-var-yeh)
dictionary

Try out your **новые слова** for that's
(noh-vih-yeh)
new

how you make them yours to use on your

holiday. Remember, the more **вы** practice
(vwee)

теперь, the more enjoyable your trip will
(tyep-yair)

be. **Удачи!**
(oo-dah-chee)
good luck

ОТВЕТЫ

1. Я говорю по-русски.
2. Мы изучаем русский.
3. Она понимает по-английски.
4. Он приезжает из Америку.
5. Они живут в Канаде.
6. Вы покупаете книгу.

(skohl-kah) *(vreh-mee-nee)*
Сколько времени?
what   time is it

(vwee)   *(kahk)*   *(dnee)* *(nee-dyel-ee)*   *(myeh-syet-sih)* *(go-dah)*
Вы know, **как** to tell **дни недели и месяцы года**, so now let's learn to tell time. As a
days (of) week   months (of)   year

(vuh)
traveler **в Россию, вы** need to be able to tell time in order to make **заказ и** to catch
(zah-kahz)
reservations

(poh-yez-dah)   *(voht)*
поезда и автобусы. Вот the "basics."
trains   buses   here are

What time is it?	=	**Сколько времени?** *(vreh-mee-nee)* _____
	=	**Который час?** *(kah-toh-ree)* *(chahs)* _____
o'clock, hour	=	**час** *(chahs)* _____
minutes	=	**минут** *(mee-noot)* _____
half	=	**половина** *(pah-lah-vee-nah)* _____
minus	=	**без** *(byez)* _____
a quarter toward	=	**четверть** *(chet-virt)* _____
a quarter from	=	**без четверти** *(byez)* *(chet-virt-ee)* _____

Теперь quiz yourself. Fill in the missing letters below.

hour = | ч | а | | minus = | б | | з | o'clock = | ч | а | |

quarter toward = | ч | е | т | | | т | ь |

half = | п | о | | о | в | | а | and finally

What time is it? | к | | т | р | ы | ✕ | ч | | с | ? |

❏ **капитал** *(kah-pee-tahl)* .... capital (money) _____
❏ — **капиталист** *(kah-pee-tah-leest)* .... capitalist _____
❏ **карамель** *(kah-rah-myel)* .... caramel   **к** _____
❏ **класс** *(klahs)* .... class _____
❏ **классик** *(klahs-seek)* .... classic _____

46

Теперь, как are these **слова** used? Study **примеры внизу**. When **вы** think it through, it

(pree-myair-ih) *(vnee-zoo)*
examples   below

really is **не** too difficult. Just notice that the pattern changes after the halfway mark.

(nyeh)
not

Through the halfway mark **вы** use the special endings **-ого** and **-его**.

(oh-vah / ah-vah) *(yeh-vah)*

(chah-sohv)
Пять часов.
o'clock

| 5.00 |

Пять часов. Пять часов.

(dyes-yet) *(mee-noot)* *(shest-oh-vah)*
Десять минут шестого.
ten   minutes (toward) sixth hour

| 5.10 |

(chet-virt)
Четверть шестого.

| 5.15 |

(dvahd-tset) *(mee-noot)* *(shest-oh-vah)*
Двадцать минут шестого.
twenty   minutes (toward) sixth hour

| 5.20 |

(pah-lah-vee-nah)
Половина шестого.
half (of)   sixth hour

| 5.30 |

(byez) *(dvahd-tset-ee)* *(shest)*
Без двадцати шесть.
minus   twenty (from)   six

| 5.40 |

Без четверти шесть.

| 5.45 |

(dyes-yet-ee)
Без десяти шесть.
ten (from)

| 5.50 |

(chah-shov)
Шесть часов.

| 6.00 |

See how **важно** learning **числа** is? **Теперь** answer the following **вопросы** based on **часах**

(chee-slah)
important   numbers

(vah-proh-sih) *(chah-sahk)*
questions   clocks

below. **Ответы** are at the bottom of **страницы. Сколько времени?**

(skohl-kah) *(vreh-mee-nee)*

1. | 8.00 | _____

2. | 7.15 | _____

3. | 4.30 | _____

4. | 9.20 | _____

ОТВЕТЫ

4. Двадцать минут десятого.   2. Четверть восьмого.
3. Половина пятого.   1. Восемь часов.

47

When **вы** *(vwee)* answer a "**когда**" *(kahg-dah)* question, say "**в**" *(vuh)* before **вы** *(vwee)* give the time. **Ответы внизу.** *(aht-vyet-ih) (vnee-zoo)*

(when) *(at)*

1. **Когда приходит поезд?** *(pree-hoh-deet) (poh-yezd)* _____
   comes — train   (at 6:00)

2. **Когда приходит автобус?** *(kahg-dah) (pree-hoh-deet) (ahv-toh-boos)* _____
   comes — bus   (at 7:30)

3. **Когда начинается концерт?** *(kahg-dah) (nah-chee-nah-yet-syah) (kahn-tsairt)* _____
   begins — concert   (at 8:00)

4. **Когда начинается фильм?** *(kahg-dah) (nah-chee-nah-yet-syah) (feelm)* _____
   begins — film   (at 9:00)

5. **Когда открывается ресторан?** *(aht-krih-vah-yet-syah) (res-tah-rahn)* _____
   opens — restaurant   (at 11:30)

6. **Когда открывается банк?** *(aht-krih-vah-yet-syah) (bahnk)* _____
   opens — bank   (at 8:30)

7. **Когда закрывается банк?** *(zah-krih-vah-yet-syah)* _____
   closes   (at 5:30)

8. **Когда закрывается ресторан?** *(zah-krih-vah-yet-syah)* _____
   closes   (at 10:30)

Вот *(voht)* a quick quiz. Fill in the blanks with the correct **числами.** *(chee-slah-mee)*

numbers

9. **В минуте** *(vuh) (mee-noot-yeh)* _____ **секунд.** *(see-koond)*
   minute (there are)   (?)   seconds

10. **В часе** *(chahs-yeh)* _____ **минут.**
    hour   (?)   minutes

11. **В неделе** *(nee-dyel-yeh)* _____ **дней.** *(dnay)*
    (?)   days

12. **В году** *(gah-doo)* _____ **месяцев.** *(myeh-syet-syev)*
    (?)   months

13. **В году** _____ **недели.** *(nee-dyel-ee)*
    (?)   weeks

14. **В году** _____ **дней.**
    (?)

ОТВЕТЫ

1. в шесть часов
2. в половине восьмого
3. в восемь часов
4. в девять часов
5. в половине двенадцатого
6. в половине девятого
7. в половине шестого
8. в половине одиннадцатого
9. шестьдесят
10. шестьдесят
11. семь
12. двенадцать
13. пятьдесят две
14. триста шестьдесят пять

48

Do **вы** remember your greetings from earlier? It is a good time to review them as they will

(oh-chen) *(vahzh-nih-yeh)*
always be **очень важные.**
very   important

(vuh) *(voh-syem)*   *(oo-trah)*   *(gah-vah-reem)* *(doh-brah-yeh)* *(oo-trah)*   *(nee-kah-lah-yev-nah)*
В восемь часов утра мы говорим "Доброе утро, Мария Николаевна."
at   in morning   say   good   morning

(shtoh) *(mwee)*
Что мы говорим? *Доброе утро, Мария Николаевна.*
what

(chahs)(den-yah) *(mwee)*   *(dyen)*   *(nee-kah-lah-yev-eech)*
В час дня мы говорим "Добрый день, Иван Николаевич."
one   in afternoon

(shtoh) *(mwee)*
Что мы говорим? _____

(chah-sohv) *(vyeh-cheh-rah)*   *(doh-brih)* *(vyeh-cher)* *(pee-trohv-nah)*
В восемь часов вечера мы говорим "Добрый вечер, Анна Петровна."
          in evening

(shtoh) *(mwee)*
Что мы говорим? _____

(dyes-yet)   *(spah-koy-nay)* *(noh-chee)* *(zee-nah-ee-dah)*
В десять часов вечера мы говорим "Спокойной ночи, Зинаида."
ten   in evening   good   night

(shtoh) *(mwee)*
Что мы говорим? _____

(pah-roos-skee)
По-русски, the letter **"е"** is often pronounced *"yeh"* (as in the English word "yes"). When a
in   Russian

letter such as **с, н, б, д** or **п** precedes the *"yeh"* sound, they can combine to make one sound.

(roos-skah-yeh)
For example, the **русское слово** for "no" is **"нет"** pronounced like "net" with a "y": *"nyet."*

As you practice each of the following words, combine the sound of *"yeh"* with the letter that

precedes it, making one, smooth sound.

(gdyeh)   *(syem)*   *(kah-bee-nyet)*
где   **семь**   **кабинет**
where   seven   study

(zdyes)   *(dyev-yet)*   *(byeh-lee)*
здесь   **девять**   **белый**
here   nine   white

(dyeh-tee)   *(dyes-yet)*   *(syeh-ree)*
дети   **десять**   **серый**
children   ten   gray

❑ **клоун** *(kloh-oon)* . . . . clown _____
❑ **коллекция** *(kahl-yekt-see-yah)* . . . . collection _____
❑ **командир** *(kah-mahn-deer)* . . . . commander **К** _____
❑ **комедия** *(kah-myeh-dee-yah)* . . . . comedy _____
❑ **комиссар** *(kah-mees-sar)* . . . . commissar _____

(noh-vih-yeh)
Вот новые verbs for Step 13.
new

(yest)
есть _____
to eat

(peet)
пить _____
to drink

(yest)
есть
to eat

(peet)
пить
to drink

(yah)   *(soop)*
Я _____ **суп.**

Он _____   *(borshch)*
Она   **борщ.**

(mnoh-gah)
Мы _____ **много.**
                                          a lot
(hlyeb)
Вы _____ **хлеб.**
                                          bread
                                          (rih-boo)
Они _____ **рыбу.**
                                          fish

                                          (soop)
Я _пью/_____ **молоко.**
                                          milk
                                          (byeh-lah-yeh) (vee-noh)
Он _____ **белое   вино.**
Она   white
                                          (pee-vah)
(mwee)
Мы _пьём/_____ **пиво.**

                                          (vah-doo)
Вы _____ **воду.**

                                          (chy)
Они _____ **чай.**
                                          tea

As **вы** have probably noticed, the sound of the Russian letter "**й**" varies greatly. Here are

some examples.

(kar-teen-koy)	*(yev-ray-kah)*	*(moo-zay)*	*(chy)*	*(syeh-ree)*
картинкой	**еврейка**	**музей**	**чай**	**серый**
picture	Jewish woman	museum	tea	gray

❏ **коммунист** *(kahm-moo-neest)* .... communist _____
❏ **компас** *(kohm-pahs)* .... compass _____
❏ **композитор** *(kahm-pah-zee-tar)* .... composer **К** _____
❏ **конференция** *(kahn-fyair-yent-see-yah)* .... conference _____
❏ **концерт** *(kahn-tsairt)* .... concert _____

(vwee)
Вы have learned a lot of material in the last few steps **и** that means it is time to quiz yourself.

Don't panic, this is just for you **и** no one else needs to know how **вы** did. Remember, this is a

chance to review, find out, *(shtoh)* **что вы** remember **и что вы** need to spend more time on. After **вы**

have finished, check your *(aht-vyet-ih)* **ответы** in the glossary at the back of this book. Circle the correct

answers.

кофе -	tea	coffee		**семья** -	seven	family
нет -	yes	no		**дети** -	children	grandfather
дядя -	aunt	uncle		**молоко** -	butter	~~milk~~
или -	and	or		**соль** -	pepper	salt
изучать -	to drink	to learn		**под** -	under	over
ночь -	morning	night		**врач** -	man	doctor
вторник -	Friday	Tuesday		**июнь** -	June	July
видеть -	to see	to look for		**религии** -	kitchen	religions
жарко -	cold	hot		**у меня есть** -	I want	I have
деньги -	money	page		**жить** -	to wait for	to live/reside
десять -	nine	ten		**завтра** -	yesterday	tomorrow
много -	many	bread		**хорошо** -	good	yellow

Как дела?   What time is it?   How are you?   Well, how are you after this quiz?

❑ **коньяк** *(kahn-yahk)* . . . . cognac
❑ **корт** *(kort)* . . . . court (tennis)
❑ **кот** *(koht)* . . . . cat (male)   **К**
❑ **краб** *(krahb)* . . . . crab
❑ **Куба** *(koo-bah)* . . . . Cuba

14

(syev-yair) *(yoog)* *(vah-stohk)* *(zah-pahd)*
Север - юг, восток - запад
north   south   east   west

(vwee) *(kar-too)* *(nyeh)*
If **вы** are looking at **карту и вы** see the following **слова**, it should **не** be too difficult to
map

(shtoh) *(ah-nee)* *(vnee-zoo)*
figure out, **что они** mean. Take an educated guess. **Ответы внизу.**
what they   below

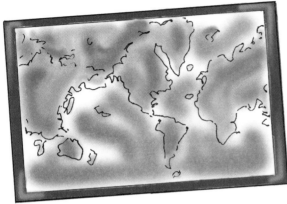

(syev-yair-nah-yah) *(dah-koh-tah)* *(yoozh-nah-yah)*
Северная Дакота   **Южная Дакота**

(ah-myeh-ree-kah)
Северная Америка   **Южная Америка**

(kah-rah-lee-nah)
Северная Каролина   **Южная Каролина**

(kah-reh-yah) *(ah-free-kah)*
Северная Корея   **Южная Африка**

(sloh-vah) *(vlah-dee-vah-stohk)*
Do **вы** recognize **русское слово** for east in **"Владивосток"?** Here it means "eastern domain."

(vlah-dee-vah-stohk)
Владивосток is the easternmost seaport in **России**. It is also the terminus of the

(mahsk-vih)
Trans-Siberian Railroad, 5700 miles east of **Москвы.**
Moscow

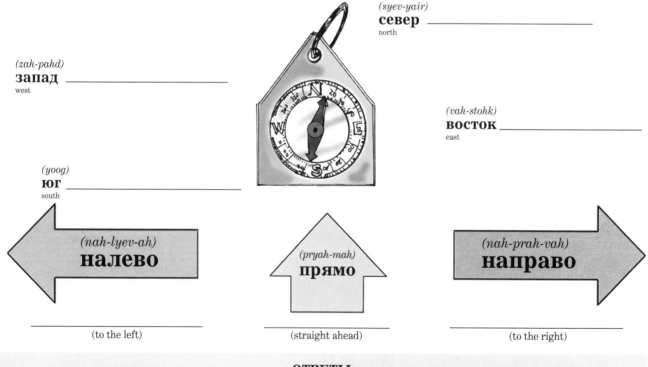

(syev-yair)
север _____
north

(zah-pahd)
запад _____
west

(vah-stohk)
восток _____
east

(yoog)
юг _____
south

(nah-lyev-ah)
налево

(pryah-mah)
прямо

(nah-prah-vah)
направо

_____   _____   _____
(to the left)   (straight ahead)   (to the right)

These **слова** can go a long way. Say them aloud each time you write them in the blanks below.

(pah-zhahl-oos-tah)
пожалуйста _____
please

(spah-see-bah)
спасибо _____
thank you

(eez-vee-neet-yeh)
извините _____
excuse me

(pah-zhahl-oos-tah)
пожалуйста _____
you're welcome

(voht) (dvah)   *(dee-ah-loh-gah) (dil-yah)*
Вот два typical **диалога для**   someone who is trying to find something. Write them out.
   two   dialogues   for

(bar-ees)   *(eez-vee-neet-yeh)*   *(gah-stee-neet-sah) (oo-krah-ee-nah)*
Борис: **Извините. Где гостиница Украина?**
         excuse me   hotel   Ukraina

_____ *Извините.   Где   гостиница   Украина?* _____

(lyen-ah)   *(prah-ee-dyoht-yeh) (doh) (oo-leet-sih) (gairt-sen-ah)*   *(nah-prah-vah)*
Лена: **Пройдёте до улицы Герцена и там направо.**
        go   to   street   there   to the right

_____

(gah-stee-neet-sah) (oo-krah-ee-nah) (nah) (oo-gloo)
Гостиница Украина на углу.
                        on   corner

_____

(ahl-yeg)   *(eez-vee-neet-yeh)*   *(moo-zay) (tahl-stoh-vah)*
Олег: **Извините. Где музей Толстого?**
        excuse me   museum   Tolstoy

_____

(ohl-gah)   *(prah-ee-dyoht-yeh) (nah-prah-vah)*   *(pah-tohm) (pryah-mah) (doh) (oo-leet-sih)*
Ольга: **Пройдёте направо; потом прямо до улицы**
        go   to the right   then   straight ahead   to   street

_____

(tahl-stoh-vah)   *(nah-lyev-ah) (moo-zay) (nah) (oo-gloo)*
Толстого. Там налево, и музей на углу.
  Tolstoy   to the left   on   corner

_____

❑ **лаборатория** *(lah-bah-rah-toh-ree-yah)* . . . . . laboratory	_____
❑ **лимон** *(lee-mohn)* . . . . lemon	_____
❑ **— лимонад** *(lee-mah-nahd)*. . . . . lemonade **Л**	_____
❑ **линия** *(lee-nee-yah)* . . . . line	_____
❑ **литература** *(lee-tyair-ah-too-rah)* . . . . literature	_____

Are **вы** *(vwee)* lost? There is no need to be lost if **вы** *(vwee)* have learned the basic direction **слова**. Do not

try to memorize these **диалоги** *(dee-ah-loh-gee)* because **вы** will never be looking for precisely these places.
dialogues

One day, **вы** might need to ask **дорогу** *(dah-roh-goo)* to the **Большой** *(bahl-shoy)* **театр**, *(tee-ah-ter)* **ГУМ** *(goom)* or **Кремль.** *(kreml)*
directions · Bolshoi · Theater · GUM Department Store · Kremlin

Learn the key direction **слова и** be sure **вы** can find your destination. **Вы** may want to buy a

guidebook to start planning which places **вы** would like to visit. Practice asking **дорогу** *(dah-roh-goo)* to
directions

these special places. What if the person responding to your **вопрос** *(vah-prohs)* answers too quickly for

вы to understand the entire reply? Practice saying,

Извините.	**Я** *(yah)*	**не** *(nyeh)*	**понимаю.** *(pah-nee-mah-yoo)*	**Пожалуйста,** *(pah-zhahl-oos-tah)*	**повторите!** *(pahv-tah-reet-yeh)*	**Спасибо.** *(spah-see-bah)*
excuse me	I	(do) not understand		please	repeat	

Теперь say it again **и** then write it out below.

_____

(Excuse me. I do not understand. Please repeat. Thank you.)

Да, *(dah)* it is difficult at first but don't give up! **Когда** *(kahg-dah)* the directions are repeated, **вы** will be able
yes · when

to understand if **вы** have learned the key **слова**. Let's review.

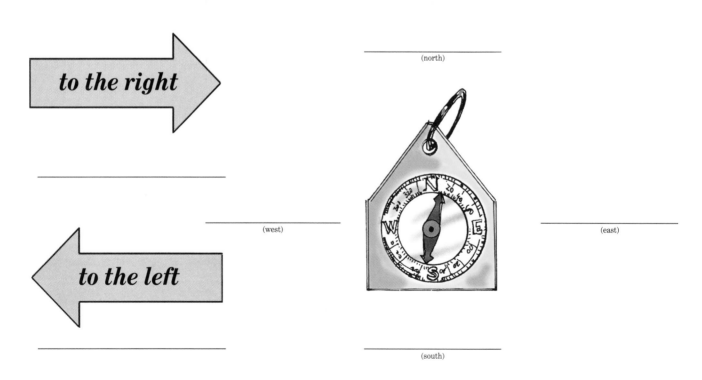

to the right

(north) _____

(west) _____   (east) _____

to the left

(south) _____

❏ **май** *(my)*	May		_____
❏ **март** *(mart)*	March		_____
❏ **масса** *(mahs-sah)*	mass	**M**	_____
❏ **мастер** *(mahs-tyair)*	master		_____
❏ **математика** *(mah-tyeh-mah-tee-kah)*	mathematics		_____

(cheh-tir-ee) *(noh-vik)*
Вот четыре новых verbs. **Они** are different from the patterns **вы** have learned, so pay close
  new   they

attention. **Вы** will probably use these verbs more than any others.

(yah) *(hah-choo)*
я хочу _____
I   would like

(men-yeh) *(noozh-nah)*
мне нужно _____
I   need

(men-yah) *(zah-voot)*
меня зовут _____
my name is

(oo) *(men-yah)* *(yest)*
у меня есть _____
I have

As always, say each sentence out loud. Say each **и** every **слово** carefully, pronouncing each

русский sound as well as **вы** can.

(yah) *(hah-choo)*
я хочу
I   would like

(bah-kahl) *(vee-nah)*
Я _____ **бокал вина.**
                           glass (of)
(mah-lah-kah)
Он _____ **стакан молока.**
Она
(mwee)
Мы _ХОТИМ /_____ **стакан воды.**
                                    (vah-dih)
(chahsh-kee) *(koh-fyeh)*
Вы _____ **две чашки кофе.**
                            cups (of)
(chah-yah)
Они _____ **три чашки чая.**
they

(men-yeh) *(noozh-nah)*
мне нужно
I   need

(men-yeh)
Мне _____ **стакан лимонада.**
                                      (stah-kahn) *(lee-mah-nah-dah)*
                                                     lemonade
(ee-moo)
Ему _____ **стакан молока.**
(yay)
Ей
(chahsh-kee) *(chah-yah)*
Нам _____ **три чашки чая.**
(vahm)
Вам _____ **две чашки чая.**
(eem)
Им _____ **три чашки какао.**
                           (kah-kah-oh)
                            cocoa

(men-yah) *(zah-voot)*
меня зовут . . .
my name is

(men-yah)
Меня _____ **Наталья.**
                             (nah-tahl-yah)
(yee-voh)
Его _____ **Олег/Ольга.**
(yee-yoh)
Её
(nahs)
Нас _____ **Борис и Лена.**
our names are   *(bar-ees)* *(lyen-ah)*
(vahs)
Вас _____ **Антон.**
your name is   *(ahn-tohn)*
(eehk)
Их _____ **Анна и Пётр.**
their names are *(ahn-nah)* *(pyoh-ter)*

(oo) *(men-yah)* *(yest)*
у меня есть
I have

(oo) *(men-yah)*
У меня _____ **пять тысяч рублей.**
                         (pyaht) *(tih-syahch)* *(roo-blay)*
(nyeh-voh)
У него _____ **шесть тысяч рублей.**
                         (shest)
(nyeh-yoh)
У неё
У нас _есть /_____ **два тысячи рублей.**
                           (dvah) *(tih-syah-chee)*
(vahs)
У вас _____ **восемь тысяч рублей.**
                        (voh-syem)
(neehk)
У них _____ **девять тысяч рублей.**
                        (dyev-yet)

❏ **материя** *(mah-tyair-ee-yah)* . . . . material _____
❏ **матч** *(mahtch)* . . . . match (game) _____
❏ **машина** *(mah-shee-nah)* . . . . machine (car) **М** _____
❏ **медаль** *(myeh-dahl)* . . . . medal _____
❏ **медик** *(myeh-deek)* . . . . medic _____

(nah-vyair-hoo)   *(vnee-zoo)*

Наверху - внизу
upstairs   downstairs, below

(tyep-yair)   *(bohl-shee)*   *(dohm)* *(vuh)* *(kee-yev-yeh)*   *(spahl-nyoo)*

Теперь let's learn **больше слов. Дом в Киеве.** Go to your **спальню и** look around the
more   Kiev   bedroom

(kohm-nah-tih)   *(spahl-nyeh)*

комнаты. Let's learn the names of the things **в спальне,** just like
room   bedroom

(mwee)   *(doh-mah)*

мы learned the various parts of **дома.**

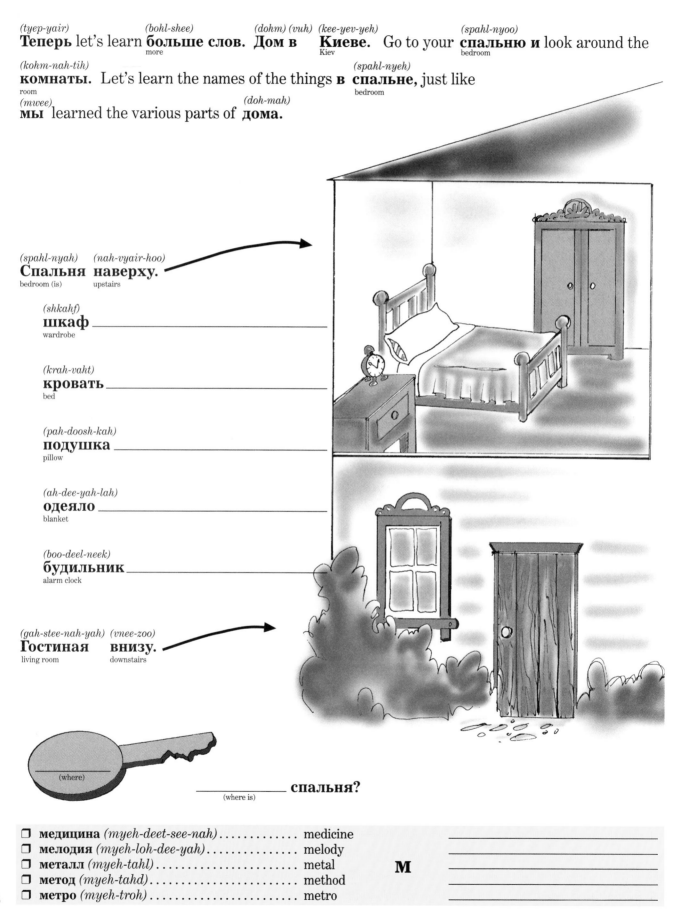

(spahl-nyah)   *(nah-vyair-hoo)*

Спальня наверху.
bedroom (is)   upstairs

(shkahf)

шкаф _____
wardrobe

(krah-vaht)

кровать _____
bed

(pah-doosh-kah)

подушка _____
pillow

(ah-dee-yah-lah)

одеяло _____
blanket

(boo-deel-neek)

будильник _____
alarm clock

(gah-stee-nah-yah)   *(vnee-zoo)*

Гостиная внизу.
living room   downstairs

_____
(where)

_____ **спальня?**
(where is)

☐ **медицина** *(myeh-deet-see-nah)* . . . . medicine   _____
☐ **мелодия** *(myeh-loh-dee-yah)* . . . . melody   _____
☐ **металл** *(myeh-tahl)* . . . . metal   **M** _____
☐ **метод** *(myeh-tahd)* . . . . method   _____
☐ **метро** *(myeh-troh)* . . . . metro   _____

Теперь, remove the next **пять** *(pyaht)* stickers **и** label these things **в** *(vuh)* your **спальне** *(spahl-nyeh)*. Let's move **в** *(into)*

ванную *(vahn-noo-yoo)* **и** do the same thing. Remember, **ванная** *(vah-nah-yah)* means a **комната** to bathe in. If **вы** *(vwee)* **в**
bathroom   room

ресторане, и вам нужно to use the lavatory, **вы** want to ask for **туалет** *(too-ahl-yet)* not for **ванная** *(vahn-nah-yah)*.
you   need

Restrooms are marked with the letters **Ж** **и** **М**. This should be easy

to remember as **М** stands for men's just as it does in English.

Ж = **женский** *(zhen-skee)*
ladies' (restroom)

М = **мужской** *(moozh-skoy)*
men's (restroom)

Ванная **тоже** **наверху.** *(vahn-nah-yah) (toh-zheh) (nah-vyair-hoo)*
bathroom   also

зеркало *(zyair-kah-lah)* _____
mirror

умывальник *(oo-mih-vahl-neek)* _____
washstand

полотенца *(pah-lah-tyent-sah)* _____
towels

туалет *(too-ahl-yet)* _____
toilet

душ *(doosh)* _____
shower

Кабинет **тоже** **внизу.** *(kah-bee-nyet) (toh-zheh) (vnee-zoo)*
study   also   downstairs

❏ **механик** *(myeh-hah-neek)*	mechanic		_____
❏ **микрофон** *(mee-krah-fohn)*	microphone		_____
❏ **миллион** *(meel-lee-ohn)*	million	**М**	_____
❏ **миниатюра** *(mee-nee-ah-tyoo-rah)*	miniature		_____
❏ **миссия** *(mees-see-yah)*	mission		_____

He *(nyeh)* forget to remove the next group of stickers **и** label these things in your **ванной.** *(vahn-noy)* _{bathroom} Okay, it is

time to review. Here's a quick quiz to see what you remember.

men's (restroom) — **внизу** *(vnee-zoo)*

I need — **мужской** *(moozh-skoy)*

downstairs — **пожалуйста** *(pah-zhahl-oos-tah)*

please — **прямо** *(pryah-mah)*

towels — **туалет** *(too-ahl-yet)*

upstairs — **женский** *(zhen-skee)*

bathroom — **полотенца** *(pah-lah-tyent-sah)*

lavatory / restroom — **наверху** *(nah-vyair-hoo)*

straight ahead — **мне нужно** *(men-yeh)(noozh-nah)*

women's (restroom) — **ванная** *(vahn-nah-yah)*

Next stop — **кабинет,** specifically **стол в кабинете.** **Что на столе?** Let's identify things
(kah-bee-nyet) study *(stohl)* desk / table *(kah-bee-nyet-yeh)* study *(shtoh)* what

which one normally finds **на столе** or strewn about **дома.**

(teh-leh-vee-zar)
телевизор
television

(kah-rahn-dahsh)
карандаш
pencil

(rooch-kah)
ручка
pen

(kahmp-yoo-tyer)
компьютер
computer

(boo-mah-gah)
бумага
paper

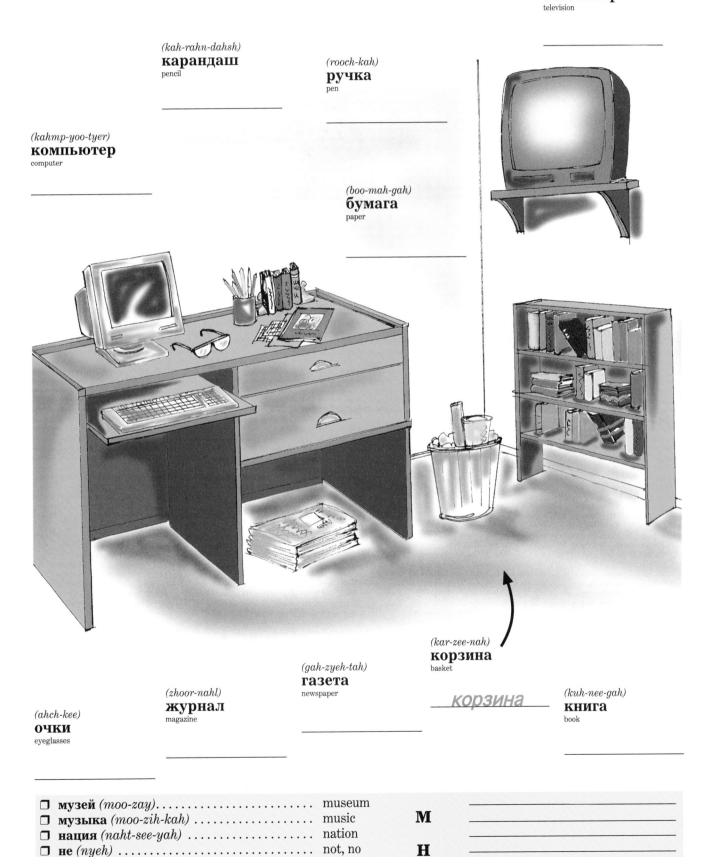

(kar-zee-nah)
корзина
basket

(gah-zyeh-tah)
газета
newspaper

(zhoor-nahl)
журнал
magazine

корзина

(kuh-nee-gah)
книга
book

(ahch-kee)
очки
eyeglasses

❏ **музей** *(moo-zay)* . . . . museum
❏ **музыка** *(moo-zih-kah)* . . . . music   **M**
❏ **нация** *(naht-see-yah)* . . . . nation
❏ **не** *(nyeh)* • . . . . not, no   **H**
❏ **— несерьёзный** *(nyeh-syair-yohz-nee)* . . . . not serious

(pees-moh)
письмо
letter

(mar-kah)
марка
stamp

(aht-krit-kah)
открытка
postcard

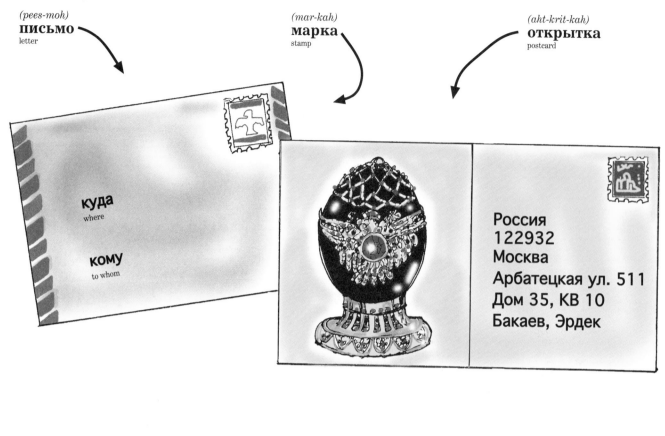

куда
where

кому
to whom

Россия
122932
Москва
Арбатецкая ул. 511
Дом 35, КВ 10
Бакаев, Эрдек

_____ (letter)

_____ (stamp)

_____ (postcard)

(ah-vee-ah)
Авиа is short for "**авиапочтой.**" *(ah-vee-ah-poach-toy)* Did **вы** notice that Russian addresses are written in
by airmail

reverse order starting with the country, zip code, street, bulding and apartment numbers

and ending with the name?

Теперь label these things **в кабинете** *(kah-bee-nyet-yeh)* with your stickers. Do not forget to say these **слова**

out loud whenever **вы** write them, **вы** see them **или вы** apply the stickers.

Remember **не** *(nyeh)* is extremely useful **по-русски.** Add **не** before a verb **и вы** negate the sentence.
not

Я хочу бокал вина.
I would like a glass wine

Я не хочу бокал вина.
I would not like a glass wine

Simple, isn't it? **Теперь,** after you fill in the blanks on the next page, go back a second time

☐ **нейлон** *(nay-lohn)* . . . . nylon
☐ **нет!** *(nyet)* . . . . no!
☐ **никель** *(neek-yehl)* . . . . nickel
☐ **норма** *(nor-mah)* . . . . norm, standard
☐ **нос** *(nohs)* . . . . nose

Н _____
_____
_____
_____

and negate all these sentences by adding **"не"** before each verb. Practice saying these sentences out loud many times. Don't get discouraged! Just look at how much **вы** have already learned **и** think ahead to **икра,** *(ee-krah)* **балет** *(bahl-yet)* **и** adventure.
caviar

(prah-dah-vaht)
продавать _____
to sell

(spaht)
спать _____
to sleep

(pah-sih-laht)
посылать _____
to send

(zvah-neet)
звонить _____
to phone

(prah-dah-vaht)
продавать
to sell

Я _____ **цветы.** *(tsvet-ih)*
flowers

Он _____ **фрукты.** *(frook-tih)*
Она fruit

Мы _____ **билеты.** *(beel-yet-ih)*

Вы _____ **много билеты.** *(mnoh-gah)* *(beel-yet-ahv)*
many

Они _____ **открытки.** *(aht-krit-kee)*

(pah-sih-laht)
посылать
to send

Я _____ **письмо.** *(pees-moh)*
letter

Он _____ **открытку.** *(aht-krit-koo)*
Она

Мы *посылаем/* _____ **книгу.** *(kuh-nee-goo)*

Вы _____ **четыре открытки.** *(cheh-tir-ee)* *(aht-krit-kee)*

Они _____ **три письма.** *(pees-mah)*

(spaht)
спать
to sleep

Я _____ **в спальне.** *(vuh)* *(spahl-nyeh)*
bedroom

Он _____ **на кровати.** *(krah-vah-tee)*
Она

Мы _____ **в гостинице.**

Вы _____ **в доме.**

Они _____ **под одеялом.** *(ah-dee-yah-lahm)*
under blanket

(zvah-neet)
звонить
to phone

Я _____ **в Петербург.** *(pyeh-tyair-boorg)*

Он _____ **в США.** *(seh-sheh-ah)*
Она U.S.A.

Мы _____ **в Канаду.** *(kah-nah-doo)*

Вы _____ **в Англию.** *(ahn-glee-yoo)*
England

Они _____ **во Владивосток.**

❑ **Норвегия** *(nar-vyeh-gee-yah)* .... Norway
❑ — where they speak **по-норвежски** *(pah-nar-vyezh-skee)* **Н** _____
❑ **ноябрь** *(nah-yah-bair)* .... November
❑ **октябрь** *(ahk-tyah-bair)* .... October **О** _____
❑ **олимпиада** *(ah-leem-pee-ah-dah)* .... Olympics

61

Before **вы** proceed with the next step, *(pah-zhahl-oos-tah)* **пожалуйста** identify all the items *(vnee-zoo)* **внизу.**

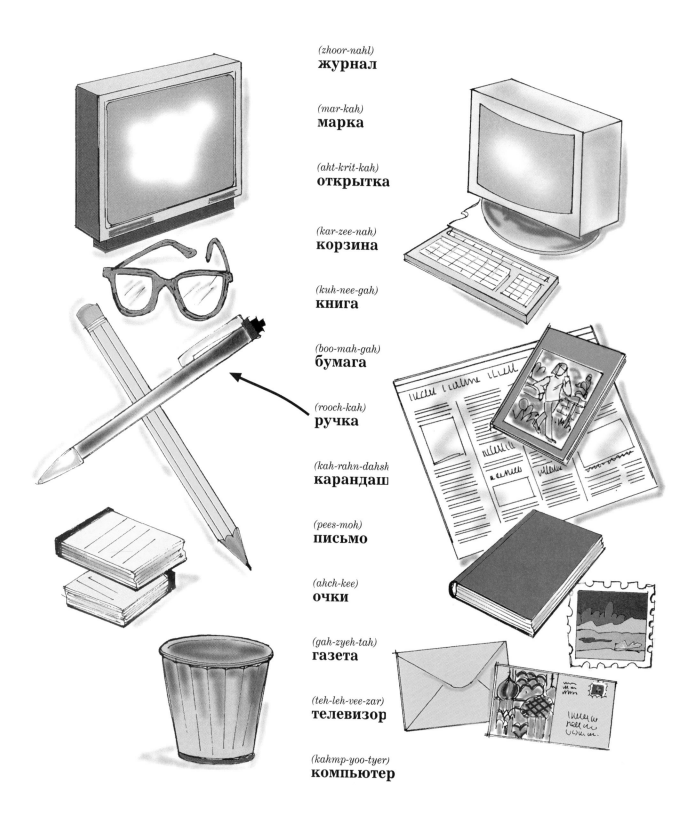

(zhoor-nahl)
журнал

(mar-kah)
марка

(aht-krit-kah)
открытка

(kar-zee-nah)
корзина

(kuh-nee-gah)
книга

(boo-mah-gah)
бумага

(rooch-kah)
ручка

(kah-rahn-dahsh)
карандаш

(pees-moh)
письмо

(ahch-kee)
очки

(gah-zyeh-tah)
газета

(teh-leh-vee-zar)
телевизор

(kahmp-yoo-tyer)
компьютер

❏ **опера** *(oh-pyair-ah)* . . . . opera
❏ **органист** *(ar-gah-neest)* . . . . organist
❏ **оркестр** *(ar-kyes-tair)* . . . . orchestra
❏ **офицер** *(ah-feet-syair)* . . . . officer
❏ **официальный** *(ah-feet-see-ahl-nee)* . . . . official

О

(vwee)   *(kahk)*   *(vah-proh-sih)*   *(suh)*
Теперь вы know, **как** to count, **как** to ask **вопросы, как** to use verbs **с** the "plug-in"

formula, **как** to make statements **и как** to describe something, be it the location of **гостиница**

(tsvet)
или цвет дома. Let's take the basics that **вы** have learned **и** expand them in special areas that
color (of)   house

(aht-krit-kee)
will be most helpful in your travels. What does everyone do on a holiday? Send **открытки,** of

(poach-tah)
course! Let's learn exactly **как почта** works because **почта в России** has everything.

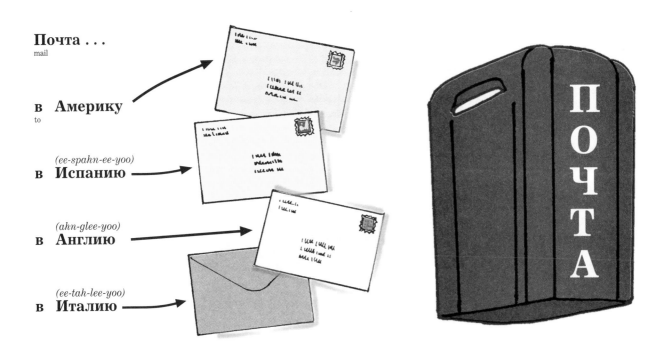

Почта . . .
mail

в Америку
to

(ee-spahn-ee-yoo)
в Испанию

(ahn-glee-yoo)
в Англию

(ee-tah-lee-yoo)
в Италию

         (mar-kee)   *(kahn-vyair-tih)*   *(pah-sil-kee)*   *(pees-mah)*   *(aht-krit-kee)*
Почта is where **вы** buy **марки и конверты,** send **посылки, письма и открытки.**
                            envelopes   packages   letters

(myezh-doo-gah-rohd-nee)   *(myezh-doo-nah-rohd-nee)*
Вы can use **междугородний и международный телефон на почте.** On
       long-distance   international

(vah-skree-syen-yahm)   *(zah-krih-tah)*
субботам и воскресеньям почта закрыта.
Saturdays   Sundays   closed

❏ **павильон** *(pah-veel-yohn)* . . . . pavilion
❏ **пакет** *(pah-kyet)* . . . . package
❏ **Пакистан** *(pah-kee-stahn)* . . . . Pakistan   **П**
❏ **парад** *(pah-rahd)* . . . . parade
❏ **парк** *(park)* . . . . park

(voht)
Вот the necessary **слова** *(dil-yah)* **для** *(poach-tih)* **почты.** Practice them aloud **и** write **слова** in the blanks.
here are   for   post office

(kahn-vyairt)
конверт
envelope

(aht-krit-kah)
открытка
postcard

(pah-sil-kah)
посылка
package

(eh-mail)
емейл
email

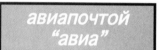

(ah-vee-ah-poach-toy)
авиапочтой
by airmail

(fahks)
факс
fax

(mar-kah)
марка
stamp

(teh-leh-fohn-ahv-tah-maht)
телефон-автомат
public telephone

(pahch-toh-vee) *(yahsh-chik)*
почтовый ящик
mailbox

(teh-leh-fohn)
телефон
telephone

Next step — **вы** ask **вопросы** like those **внизу**, depending on what **вы** **хотите**. Repeat these

(hah-teet-yeh)
would like

sentences aloud many times.

(mah-goo) *(koo-peet)* *(mar-kee)*
Где я могу купить марки? _____
I   can   buy

(aht-krit-koo)
Где я могу купить открытку? _____

Где телефон? _____

(pahch-toh-vee) *(yahsh-chik)*
Где почтовый ящик? _____
mailbox

Где телефон-автомат? _____
public telephone

(pah-slaht) *(pah-sil-koo)*
Где я могу послать посылку? _____
package

(pahz-vah-neet) *(seh-sheh-ah)*
Где я могу позвонить в США? _____
U.S.A.

(stoy-eet)
Сколько это стоит? _____
costs

Теперь, quiz yourself. Can **вы** can translate the following thoughts **на русский**?

1. Where is a public telephone? _____

2. Where can I phone to the U.S.A.? _____

3. Where can I phone to St. Petersburg? _____

4. Where is the post office? _____

5. Where can I buy stamps? _____

6. Airmail envelopes? _____

7. Where can I send a package? _____

8. Where can I send a fax? _____

(voht)
Вот are more verbs.

(die-tee) (men-yeh)
дайте мне _____
give   me

(pee-saht)
писать _____
to write

(pah-kah-zih-vaht)
показывать _____
to show

(zah-plah-teet) (zah)
заплатить за _____
to pay

Practice these verbs by not only filling in the blanks, but by saying them aloud many, many

times until you are comfortable with the sounds and the words.

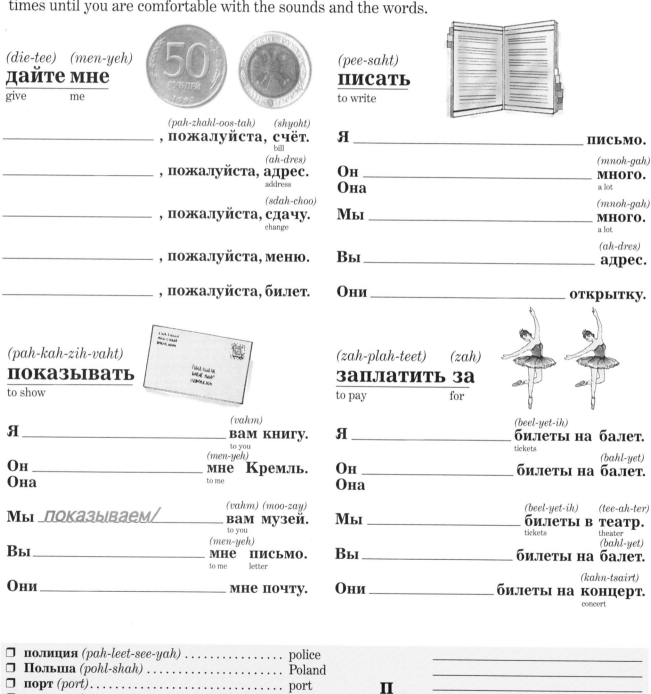

(die-tee) (men-yeh)
дайте мне
give   me

(pee-saht)
писать
to write

_____ *(pah-zhahl-oos-tah) (shyoht)*
, пожалуйста, счёт.
bill

Я _____ письмо.

_____ *(ah-dres)*
, пожалуйста, адрес.
address

Он _____ *(mnoh-gah)*
Она   много.
a lot

_____ *(sdah-choo)*
, пожалуйста, сдачу.
change

Мы _____ *(mnoh-gah)*
много.
a lot

_____ , пожалуйста, меню.

Вы _____ *(ah-dres)*
адрес.

_____ , пожалуйста, билет.

Они _____ открытку.

(pah-kah-zih-vaht)
показывать
to show

(zah-plah-teet) (zah)
заплатить за
to pay   for

Я _____ *(vahm)*
вам книгу.
to you

Я _____ *(beel-yet-ih)*
билеты на балет.
tickets

Он _____ *(men-yeh)*
Она   мне Кремль.
to me

Он _____ *(bahl-yet)*
Она   билеты на балет.

Мы *показываем/* _____ *(vahm) (moo-zay)*
вам музей.
to you

Мы _____ *(beel-yet-ih) (tee-ah-ter)*
билеты в театр.
tickets   theater

Вы _____ *(men-yeh)*
мне письмо.
to me   letter

Вы _____ *(bahl-yet)*
билеты на балет.

Они _____ мне почту.

Они _____ *(kahn-tsairt)*
билеты на концерт.
concert

❏ **полиция** *(pah-leet-see-yah)* . . . . police
❏ **Польша** *(pohl-shah)* . . . . Poland
❏ **порт** *(port)* . . . . port
❏ **портрет** *(part-ryet)* . . . . portrait
❏ **программа** *(prah-grahm-mah)* . . . . program

П

_____
_____
_____
_____

Some of these signs you probably recognize, but take a couple of minutes to review them anyway.

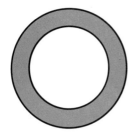

(dvee-zhen-ee-yeh) *(zah-presh-chen-oh)*
движение   запрещено
road closed to vehicles

(tah-mohzh-nyah)
таможня
customs

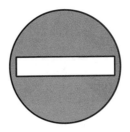

(vyezd)   *(zah-presh-chyohn)*
въезд запрещён
no entrance

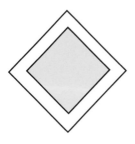

(glahv-nah-yah) *(dah-roh-gah)*
главная   дорога
main road, you have the right of way

(oo-stoo-peet-yet) *(dah-roh-goo)*
уступите дорогу
yield

(mahk-see-mahl-nah-yah) *(skoh-rahst)*
максимальная   скорость
speed limit

(stah-yahn-kah) *(zah-presh-chen-ah)*
стоянка   запрещена
no parking

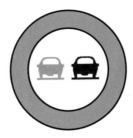

(ahb-gohn) *(zah-presh-chyohn)*
обгон запрещён
no passing

(stohp)
стоп
stop

(ahb-yezd)
ОБЪЕЗД
detour

What follows are approximate conversions, so when you order something by liters, kilograms or grams you will have an idea of what to expect and not find yourself being handed one piece of candy when you thought you ordered an entire bag.

To Convert		Do the Math		
liters (l) to gallons,	multiply by 0.26	4 liters x 0.26	=	1.04 gallons
gallons to liters,	multiply by 3.79	10 gal. x 3.79	=	37.9 liters
kilograms (kg) to pounds,	multiply by 2.2	2 kilograms x 2.2	=	4.4 pounds
pounds to kilos,	multiply by 0.46	10 pounds x 0.46	=	4.6 kg
grams (g) to ounces,	multiply by 0.035	100 grams x 0.035	=	3.5 oz.
ounces to grams,	multiply by 28.35	10 oz. x 28.35	=	283.5 g.
meters (m) to feet,	multiply by 3.28	2 meters x 3.28	=	6.56 feet
feet to meters,	multiply by 0.3	6 feet x 0.3	=	1.8 meters

For fun, take your weight in pounds and convert it into kilograms. It sounds better that way, doesn't it? How many kilometers is it from your home to school, to work, to the post office?

The Simple Versions		
one liter	=	approximately one US quart
four liters	=	approximately one US gallon
one kilo	=	approximately 2.2 pounds
100 grams	=	approximately 3.5 ounces
500 grams	=	slightly more than one pound
one meter	=	slightly more than three feet

The distance between **Москва и Петербург** is approximately 400 miles. How many kilometers would that be?

kilometers (km.) to miles,	multiply by 0.62	1000 km. x 0.62	=	620 miles
miles to kilometers,	multiply by 1.6	1000 miles x 1.6	=	1,600 km.

Inches	1	2	3	4	5	6	7

To convert centimeters into inches, multiply by 0.39   Example: 9 cm. x 0.39   = 3.51 in.

To convert inches into centimeters, multiply by 2.54   Example: 4 in. x 2.54   = 10.16 cm.

cm 1	2	3	4	5	6	7	8	9	10	11	12	13	14	15	16	17	18

18

(kahk) *(plah-teet)*
Как платить
how   to pay

(shyeh-tah)
Да, there are also **счета** to pay **в России. Вы** have just finished your delicious dinner **и**
bills

(hah-teet-yeh) *(shyoht)* *(mohzh-yet-yeh)* *(ah-feet-see-ahn-tah)*
вы хотите счёт. Как вы можете платить? Вы call for **официанта: "Официант!"**
would like   bill   can   pay   waiter

(ah-feet-see-ahnt)
Официант will normally reel off what **вы** have eaten while writing rapidly. **Он** will then
waiter

(shyoht) *(stohl)* *(roo-blay)* *(ah-feet-see-ahn-too)*
place **счёт на стол** "**Вот счёт. Восемьсот тысяч рублей.**" **Вы** will pay **официанту или**

(kahs-see-roo)
perhaps **вы** will pay **кассиру.**

(mwee) *(seh-sheh-ah)*
Being a seasoned traveler, **вы** know that tipping as **мы** know it **в США и Канаде** can vary

(shyoht-yeh)
from country to country. If the service is not included **в счёте,** round the bill up **или** simply

(ah-feet-see-ahn-tah)
leave what you consider an appropriate amount for your **официанта.** When **вы** dine out **в**

(res-tah-rahn)
России, always make a reservation. It can be very difficult to get into a popular **ресторан.**

Nevertheless, the experience is well worth the trouble **вы** will encounter to obtain a reservation.

И remember, **вы** know enough **русский** to make a reservation. Just speak slowly and clearly.

❏ **прогресс** *(prahg-ryes)* . . . . progress		_____
❏ **продукт** *(prah-dookt)* . . . . product		_____
❏ **проект** *(prah-yekt)* . . . . project	**П**	_____
❏ **профессия** *(prah-fyes-see-yah)* . . . . profession		_____
❏ **профессор** *(prah-fyes-sar)* . . . . professor		_____

Remember these key **слова** when dining out **в России.**

(ah-feet-see-ahnt)
официант _____
waiter

(ah-feet-see-ahnt-kah)
официантка _____
waitress

(shyoht)
счёт _____
bill

(sdah-chah)
сдача _____
change

(men-yoo)
меню *меню, меню, меню*
menu

(kvee-tahn-tsee-yah)
квитанция _____
receipt

(eez-vee-neet-yeh)
извините _____
excuse me

(spah-see-bah)
спасибо _____
thank you

(pah-zhahl-oos-tah)
пожалуйста _____
please

(die-tee) (men-yeh)
дайте мне _____
give   me

Вот a sample conversation involving paying *(shyoht)* **счёт.** Practice by writing it in the blanks.

(zee-nah)
Зина:

(ah-plah-teet)
Извините. Я хочу оплатить счёт.
to pay

_____

(ahd-mee-nee-strah-tor)
Администратор:

(nohm-yair) (pah-zhahl-oos-tah)
Номер, пожалуйста?
number (room)

_____

Зина:

(nohm-yair) (tree-stah) (dyes-yet)
Номер триста десять.
number

_____

Администратор:

(ahd-noo)
Спасибо. Одну минуту.

_____

Администратор: **Вот счёт.**

_____

If **вы** have any problems **с числами,** *(chee-slah-mee)* just ask someone to write out **числа,** *(chee-slah)* so that **вы** can be
numbers

sure you understand everything correctly, **Пожалуйста, напишите сумму. Спасибо.** *(nah-pee-sheet-yeh) (soom-moo)*
write out   (the) sum

Practice:_____
(Please write out the sum. Thank you.)

❏ **процент** *(praht-syent)* . . . . percent		_____
❏ **радио** *(rah-dee-oh)*. . . . . radio	**п**	_____
❏ **ракета** *(rah-kyet-ah)* . . . . rocket		_____
❏ **ранг** *(rahng)* . . . . rank	**р**	_____
❏ **рапорт** *(rah-port)* . . . . report		_____

Теперь, let's take a break from *(shyeh-tohv)* **счетов и** *(dyen-yeg)* **денег** и learn some *(noh-vih-yeh)* **новые** fun **слова. Вы** can

money — new

always practice these **слова** by using your flash cards at the back of this *(kuh-nee-gah)* **книга.** Carry these

flash cards in your purse, pocket, briefcase **или** knapsack **и** *use them!*

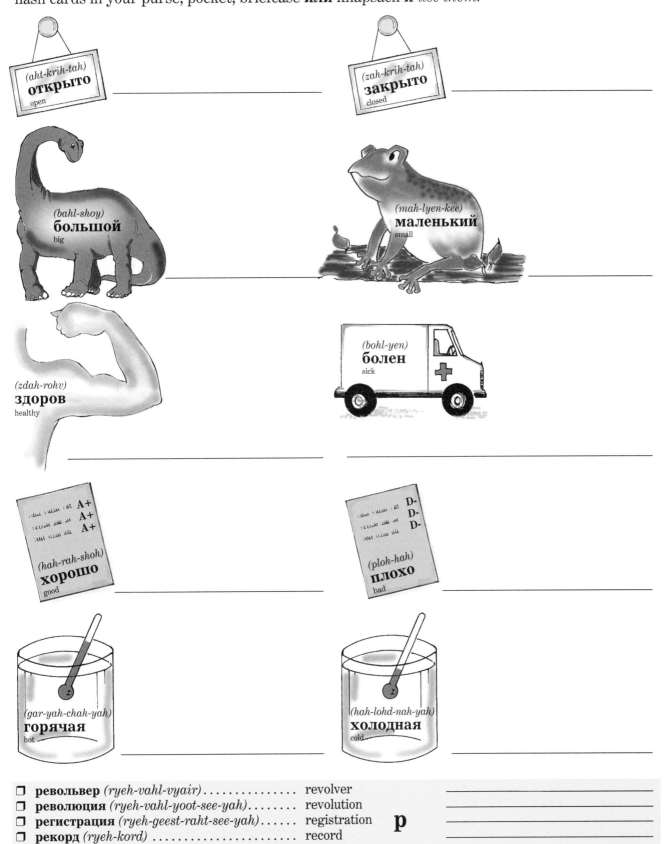

(aht-krih-tah)
открыто
open

(zah-krih-tah)
закрыто
closed

(bahl-shoy)
большой
big

(mah-lyen-kee)
маленький
small

(zdah-rohv)
здоров
healthy

(bohl-yen)
болен
sick

(hah-rah-shoh)
хорошо
good

(ploh-hah)
плохо
bad

(gar-yah-chah-yah)
горячая
hot

(hah-lohd-nah-yah)
холодная
cold

❑ **револьвер** *(ryeh-vahl-vyair)* . . . . revolver
❑ **революция** *(ryeh-vahl-yoot-see-yah)* . . . . revolution
❑ **регистрация** *(ryeh-geest-raht-see-yah)* . . . . . . registration **р**
❑ **рекорд** *(ryeh-kord)* . . . . record
❑ **религия** *(ree-lee-gee-yah)* . . . . religion

71

(kah-roht-kah-yah)
короткая _____
short

(dleen-nah-yah)
длинная _____
long

(myed-lyen-nah)
медленно _____
slow

(bis-trah)
быстро _____
fast

(vwee-soh-kah-yah)
высокая _____
tall

(mah-lyen-kah-yah)
маленькая _____
short, small

(stah-ree)
старый _____
old

(mah-lah-doy)
молодой _____
young

(dah-rah-gah-yah)
дорогая _____
expensive

(dyeh-shyoh-vah-yah)
дешёвая _____
inexpensive

(bah-gaht)
богат _____
rich

(byed-yen)
беден _____
poor

(mnoh-gah)
много _____
a lot

(mah-lah)
мало _____
a little

❏ **салат** *(sah-laht)* . . . . salad _____
❏ **самовар** *(sah-mah-var)* . . . . samovar _____
❏ **сезон** *(syeh-zone)* . . . . season   **с** _____
❏ **секунда** *(see-koon-dah)* . . . . second _____
❏ **семинар** *(syem-ee-nar)* . . . . seminar _____

Вот новые verbs.

(znaht)
знать _____
to know (fact, address)

(mohch)
мочь   *МОЧЬ, МОЧЬ, МОЧЬ*
to be able to, can

(chee-taht)
читать _____
to read

(poot-yeh-shest-vah-vaht)
путешествовать _____
to travel

Study the patterns **внизу** closely, as **вы** will use these verbs a lot.

(znaht)
знать
to know

Ул. Памирская

Я _____ *(vsyoh)* **всё.**
everything

Он _____ *(ah-dres)* **адрес.**
Она   address

Мы _____, как *(gah-vah-reet)* **говорить по-русски.**
how   to speak

Вы _____ *(nahz-vah-nee-yeh)* **название гостиницы.**
name

Они _____ *(res-tah-rah-nah)* **название ресторана.**

(mohch)
мочь
to be able to, can

Меня зовут Елизавета.

Я _____ *(gah-vah-reet)* **говорить по-русски.**
speak

Он _____ *(pah-nee-maht)* **понимать по-английски.**
Она   understand

Мы _____ **понимать по-русски.**

Вы _____ **говорить по-английски.**

Они _____ **говорить по-русски** *(toh-zheh)* **тоже.**
also

(chee-taht)
читать
to read

Я _____ **книгу.**

Он _____ **журнал.**
Она   magazine

Мы _____ **меню.**

Вы _____ **много.**
a lot

Они _____ **газету.**
newspaper

(poot-yeh-shest-vah-vaht)
путешествовать
to travel

Я _____ *(vuh)* **в** *(yahn-var-yeh)* **январе.**
January

Он _____ *(zee-moy)* **зимой.**
Она   in winter

Мы _____ **в** *(ee-yool-yeh)* **июле.**
July

Вы _____ *(lyet-ahm)* **летом.**
in summer

Они _____ *(vees-noy)* **весной.**
in spring

Some verbs change slightly by adding a **"за-" или "по-."** Don't panic. This does not change the basic meaning of the word. **Вот два** examples. Learn to listen for the core of the verb. For example, note the word **"платить"** within **"заплатить за."**

(plah-teet)	*(ah-plah-teet)*	*(zah-plah-teet)*	*(zah)*
платить — оплатить — заплатить за			
to pay	to pay	to pay	for

Я *(plah-choo)* **плачу** пять тысяч рублей.

Я **хочу оплатить** *(shyoht)* **счёт.**

Я *(zah-plah-choo)* **заплачу за** *(ah-byed)* **обед.**
         meal

(koo-peet)	*(pah-koo-paht)*
купить — покупать	
to buy	to buy

Я **хочу купить** *(mar-kee)* **марки.**

Я **хочу купить** *(kuh-nee-goo)* **книгу.**

Я **покупаю** *(pah-koo-pah-yoo) (zhoor-nahl)* **журнал.**

Вы *(mohzh-yet-yeh)* **можете** translate the sentences **внизу на русский? Ответы внизу.**
    can   into

1. I can speak Russian. _____

2. They can pay the bill. _____

3. He needs to pay the bill. _____

4. We know the address. _____ *Мы знаем адрес.* _____

5. She knows a lot. _____

6. We can read Russian. _____

7. I can pay the bill. _____

8. We are not able to (cannot) understand English. _____

9. I would like to go to Russia. _____

10. She reads the newspaper. _____

Теперь, draw *(lee-nee-yoo)* **линию** *(myezh-doo)* **между** the opposites **внизу.** **Не** forget to say them out loud. Use

(et-tee) **эти слова** every day to describe *(vesh-chee)* **вещи в доме, в** *(shkohl-yeh)* **школе, и** at work.

(vwee-soh-kah-yah)
высокая

(nah-lyev-ah)
налево

(mah-lah-doy)
молодой

(byed-yen)
беден

(zdah-rohv)
здоров

(dleen-nah-yah)
длинная

(mnoh-gah)
много

(hah-rah-shoh)
хорошо

(gar-yah-chah-yah)
горячая

(pohd)
под

(myed-lyen-nah)
медленно

(dah-rah-gah-yah)
дорогая

(bahl-shoy)
большой

(mah-lyen-kee)
маленький

(nahd)
над

(kah-roht-kah-yah)
короткая

(dyeh-shyoh-vah-yah)
дешёвая

(mah-lah)
мало

(bohl-yen)
болен

(stah-ree)
старый

(bis-trah)
быстро

(nah-prah-vah)
направо

(hah-lohd-nah-yah)
холодная

(bah-gaht)
богат

(ploh-hah)
плохо

(mah-lyen-kah-yah)
маленькая

Теперь вы знаете, что "большой" means "large" **по-русски.** Have **вы** heard of the famous

"Большой театр"? In addition to being one of the world's foremost ballet companies, it is also

(star-yeh-shee)
старейший московский театр. It is a must to see, **когда вы** are **в Москве.**
oldest

If **вы** travel **в Петербург, тогда** visit **"Мариинский театр,"** *(mah-reen-skee)* formerly **"Театр Кирова,"** *(kee-rah-vah)* where

traditional opera and ballet productions are staged.

❏ **старт** *(start)*	start		
❏ **студент** *(stoo-dyent)*	student	**с**	
❏ **суп** *(soop)*	soup		
❏ **табак** *(tah-bahk)*	tobacco	**т**	
❏ **такси** *(tahk-see)*	taxi		

(poot-yeh-shest-vah-vaht)
Путешествовать
to travel

(vchee-rah) *(pyeh-tyair-boorg-yeh)*
Вчера в Петербурге!
yesterday

(see-vohd-nyah) *(nohv-gah-rahd-yeh)*
Сегодня в Новгороде!
today

(zahv-trah) *(smahl-yensk-yeh)*
Завтра в Смоленске!
yesterday

If you know a few key **слова**, traveling can be easy **в России**. **Россия и** the nations of the

Commonwealth of Independent States span almost 6,000 miles which is equivalent to the

(myezh-doo)
distance **между** California **и** France. **Россия** has **одиннадцать** time zones. The map below
between
(ah-deen-nud-tset)

should give you a rough idea of the size of this area and help you to understand why traveling **в**

России can be a major undertaking.

(yed-yet)
Иван едет на машине.
Ivan   goes

(poh-yezd-yeh)
Нина едет на поезде.
goes   train

(lee-teet) *(sah-mahl-yoht-yeh)*
Борис летит на самолёте.
flies   airplane

(myeh-troh)
Зина едет на метро.
subway

(ee-ree-nah) *(mah-tah-tsee-kul-yeh)*
Ирина едет на мотоцикле.
motorcycle

(veek-tor)
Виктор едет на автобусе.

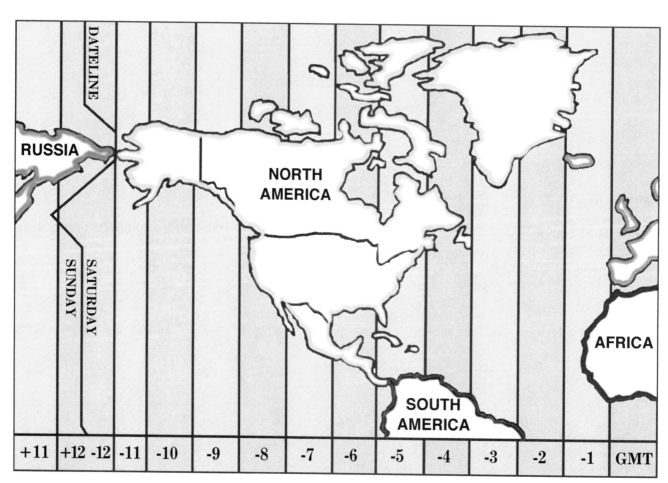

+11	+12	-12	-11	-10	-9	-8	-7	-6	-5	-4	-3	-2	-1	GMT

When **вы** are traveling, **вы** will want to tell others your nationality **и вы** will meet people from all corners of the world. Can you guess where someone is from if they say one of the following?

Ответы are in your glossary beginning on page 108.

(ah-zyair-by-dzah-nyets)
Я азербайджанец. _____

(ah-myeh-ree-kah-nyets)
Я американец. _____

(ar-myah-neen)
Я армянин. _____

(ahn-glee-chah-neen)
Я англичанин. _____

(byeh-lah-roos)
Я белорус. *Я белорус. Я белорус.*

(kah-nah-dyets)
Я канадец. _____

(es-toh-nyets)
Я эстонец. _____

(groo-zeen)
Я грузин. _____

(kah-zahk)
Я казах. _____

(kir-geez)
Я кыргыз. _____

(lah-tish)
Я латыш. _____

(lee-toh-vyets)
Я литовец. _____

(mahl-dah-vah-neen)
Я молдованин. _____

(roos-skee)
Я русский. _____

(tahd-zheek)
Я таджик. _____

(toork-myen)
Я туркмен. _____

(oo-kry-nyets)
Я украинец. _____

(ooz-bek)
Я узбек. _____

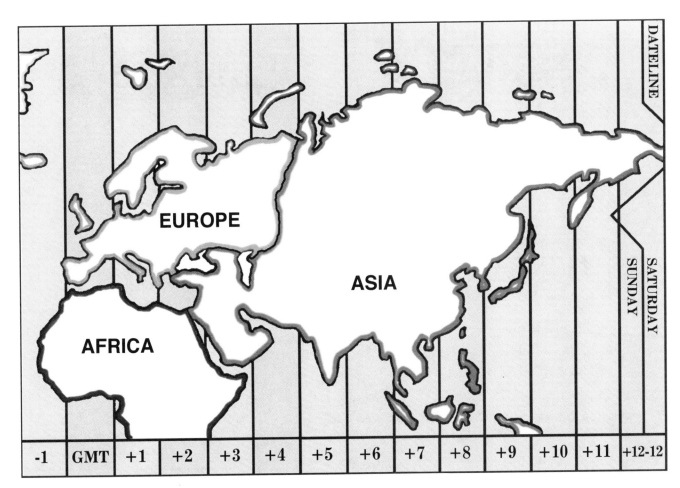

| -1 | GMT | +1 | +2 | +3 | +4 | +5 | +6 | +7 | +8 | +9 | +10 | +11 | +12-12 |

(loob-yaht) *(poot-yeh-shest-vah-vaht)* *(nyeh)*
Русские любят путешествовать. It should **не** be a surprise to find **много слов** revolving
love

(hah-teet-yeh)
around the concept of travel which is exactly what **вы хотите** to do. Practice the following
want

(chah-stah)
слова many times. **Вы** will see them **часто.**
often

(poot-yeh-shest-vah-vaht)
путешествовать _____
to travel

(byoo-roh) *(poot-yeh-shest-vee-ee)*
бюро путешествий _____
travel agency

(poot-yeh-shest-vyen-neek)
путешественник _____
traveler

(pah-yezd-kah)
поездка _____
journey, trip

If **вы** choose **ехать на машине, вот** a few key **слов.**

(shahs-syeh)
шоссе *шоссе, шоссе, шоссе*
main road

(mah-shee-nah) *(nah-prah-kaht)*
машина напрокат _____
rental car

(dah-roh-gah)
дорога _____
road

(byoo-roh) *(prah-kah-tah)*
бюро проката _____
rental agency

(oo-leet-sah)
улица _____
street

(ahv-tah-stahnt-see-yah)
автостанция _____
service station

(vnee-zoo) *(vahm)* *(noozh-nah)* *(znaht)*
Внизу some basic signs which **вам нужно знать.**
to know

(vhah-deet)
входить _____
to enter

(vwee-hah-deet)
выходить _____
to exit

ВХОД →

ВЫХОД →

(vhohd)
вход _____
entrance

(vwee-hahd)
выход _____
exit

(glahv-nee)
главный вход _____
main   entrance

(zah-pahs-noy)
запасной выход _____
emergency   exit

ОТ СЕБЯ

К СЕБЕ

(aht) *(syeb-yah)*
от себя _____
push   (doors)

(kuh) *(syeb-yeh)*
к себе _____
pull   (doors)

❑ **театр** *(tee-ah-ter)* . . . . theater _____
❑ **телевизор** *(teh-leh-vee-zar)* . . . . television _____
❑ **телеграмма** *(teh-leh-grahm-mah)* . . . . telegram   **Т** _____
❑ **телескоп** *(teh-leh-skope)*. . . . . telescope _____
78 ❑ **телефон** *(teh-leh-fohn)* . . . . telephone _____

Let's learn the basic travel verbs. Take out a piece of paper **и** make up your own sentences

with these new **слова.** Follow the same pattern **вы** have in previous Steps.

(lee-tyet)
лететь _____
to fly

(yek-haht) (nah) (mah-shee-nyeh)
ехать на машине _____
to drive

(pree-hah-deet)
приходить _____
to arrive (vehicles)

(aht-hah-deet)
отходить _____
to depart (vehicles)

(oo-yez-zhaht)
уезжать _____
to leave

(oo-klah-dih-vaht)
укладывать _____
to pack

(dyeh-laht)
делать _____
to make

(dyeh-laht) (pyair-yeh-sahd-koo)
делать пересадку _____
to transfer

Вот some *(noh-vih-yeh)* **новые** *(dil-yah)* **слова** *(pah-yezd-kee)* **для поездки.**
journey

(ah-air-ah-port)
аэропорт
airport

(plaht-for-mah)
платформа
platform

(rah-spee-sah-nee-yeh)
расписание поездов
timetable

Санкт-Петербург	---	Москва
Отправление	Поезд	Прибытие
00:41	50	12:41
07:40	19	19:40
12:15	10	00:15
14:32	04	02:32
21:40	22	09:40

(vahk-zahl)
вокзал
train station

❐ **теннис** *(tyen-nees)* . . . . tennis
❐ **три** *(tree)* . . . . three
❐ **томат** *(tah-maht)* . . . . tomato   **т**   _____
❐ **тост** *(toast)* . . . . toast
❐ **турист** *(too-reest)* . . . . tourist

C these words **вы** are ready for any trip, anywhere. **Вы** should have no problem **с** these verbs, just remember the basic "plug-in" formula **вы** have already learned. Use that knowledge to translate the following thoughts **на русский**. **Ответы внизу**. *Hint:* If **вы** have forgotten the words for "to reserve" **и** "to arrive," review pages 40 **и** 42 again.

1. I fly to Russia. _____
2. I make a transfer in Moscow. _____
3. He arrives in Yalta. _____
4. We leave tomorrow. _____ *Мы уезжаем завтра.* _____
5. We reserve tickets to Kiev. _____
6. They drive to Novgorod. _____
7. Where is the train to Odessa? _____
8. How can I fly to Russia? On British Airways or Aeroflot? _____
_____

Вот some **очень** important words for the traveler.

Санкт-Петербург	---	Москва
Отправление	Поезд	Прибытие
00:41	50	12:41
07:40	19	19:40
12:15	10	00:15
14:32	04	02:32
21:40	22	09:40

(zahn-yah-tah)
занято _____
occupied

(svah-bohd-nah)
свободно _____
free

(vah-gohn)
вагон _____
compartment, wagon

(myes-tah)
место _____
seat, place

(aht-prahv-lyen-ee-yeh)
отправление _____
departure

(pree-bit-ee-yeh)
прибытие _____
arrival

(ee-nah-strahn-nee)
иностранный _____
foreign

(myes-nee)
местный _____
domestic, internal

Increase your travel **слова** by writing out **слова внизу и** practicing the sample sentences out
loud. Practice asking **"где"** questions. It will help you **позже.** *(pohzh-yeh)*
later

(vuh)
в _____
to

Где поезд в Москву?

(poot)
путь _____
line, route

Где путь номер семь?

(kah-myair-ah) *(hrah-nyen-ee-yah)*
камера   хранения _____
left-luggage office

Где камера хранения?

(nah-seel-shcheek)
носильщик _____
porter

Где носильщик?

(sprah-vahch-nah-yeh) *(byoo-roh)*
справочное   бюро _____
information bureau

Где справочное бюро?

(tah-mohzh-nyah)
таможня _____ *Где   таможня? Где таможня?*
customs

Где таможня?

(kahs-sah)
касса _____
ticket office, cashier

Где касса?

(myes-tah)
место _____
seat, place

Это место занято?

(vah-gohn)
вагон _____
compartment, wagon

Этот вагон свободен?

(vah-gohn-res-tah-rahn)
вагон-ресторан _____
dining compartment

Где вагон-ресторан?

(spahl-nee)
спальный   вагон _____
sleeping   compartment

Где спальный вагон?

(boo-fyet)
буфет _____
snack car

Где буфет?

_____ (when) _____ (when) _____ **касса открыта?**

_____ (what) _____ (what) _____ **вы делаете?**

Вы можете *(mohzh-yet-yeh)* **прочитать** *(prah-chee-taht)* the following paragraph?
can   read

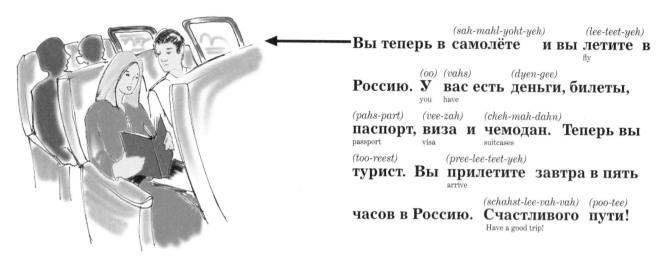

Вы теперь в самолёте *(sah-mahl-yoht-yeh)* **и вы летите в** *(lee-teet-yeh)*
fly

Россию. У *(oo)* **вас** *(vahs)* **есть деньги, билеты,** *(dyen-gee)*
you   have

паспорт, виза *(pahs-part)* *(vee-zah)* **и чемодан.** *(cheh-mah-dahn)* **Теперь вы**
passport   visa   suitcases

турист. *(too-reest)* **Вы прилетите** *(pree-lee-teet-yeh)* **завтра в пять**
arrive

часов в Россию. Счастливого *(schahst-lee-vah-vah)* **пути!** *(poo-tee)*
Have a good trip!

В России there are different types of trains – **пригородные** *(pree-gah-rahd-nee-yeh)* **поезда** called " **электрички** " *(el-ek-treech-kee)*
suburban

provide the main transportation from **пригородов** *(pree-gah-rah-dahv)* to **центра** *(tsen-trah)* **города;** *(go-rah-dah)* **междугородные** *(myezh-doo-gah-rohd-nee-yeh)*
suburbs   center (of)   city   inter-city

поезда travel longer distances **между городами.** *(gah-rah-dah-mee)* If **вы** travel **из Москвы в Петербург или**
cities   from

из Москвы во Владивосток, вы may wish to catch an express train which would travel faster

и make fewer intermediate stops.

❑ **фрукт** *(frookt)*	fruit	**ф**	_____
❑ **футбол** *(foot-bohl)*	soccer, football		_____
❑ **царь** *(tsar)*	czar, tsar	**ц**	_____
❑ **цирк** *(tseerk)*	circus		_____
❑ **Чили** *(chee-lee)*	Chile	**ч**	_____

Knowing these travel **слова** will make your holiday twice as enjoyable **и** at least three times as easy. Review these **новые слова** by doing the crossword puzzle **внизу.** *(vnee-zoo)* Drill yourself on this Step by selecting other destinations **и** ask your own **вопросы** *(vah-proh-sih)* about **поездах,** *(poh-yez-dahk)* **автобусах** *(ahv-toh-boo-sahk)* **или** **самолётах** *(sah-mahl-yoh-tahk)* that go there. Select **новые слова из словаря** *(slah-var-yah)* **и** ask your own questions from beginning with **где, когда,** and **сколько стоит. Ответы** to the crossword puzzle are at the bottom of the next page. **Удачи!**

ACROSS

1. to arrive
2. page
3. platform
4. excuse me
5. main road
6. compartment
7. to eat
8. one
9. thank-you
10. why
11. east
13. customs
14. trip, journey
15. fast
16. domestic, internal
17. to order, to reserve
18. street
19. bank
20. motorcycle

DOWN

3. traveler
8. departure
14. to drink
16. menu
21. restaurant
22. Jewish man
23. or
24. tomorrow
25. over
26. timetable
27. airport
28. hour, o'clock
30. open
31. porter
32. give!
33. taxi
34. toilet

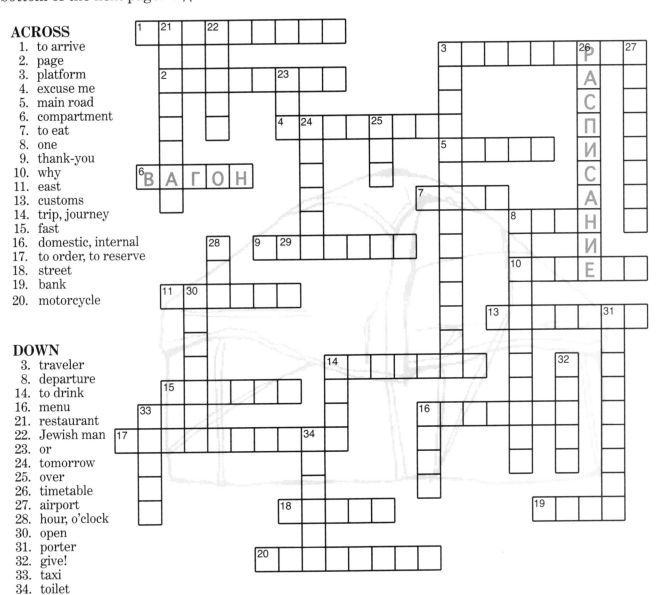

юрта – yurt, the traditional nomadic 'home' of Central Asia. The flag of the Kyrgyzstan depicts a birds-eye view of these felt-covered structures which have no sharp edges and protect their owners from the harsh elements throughout the year.

❏ **шарф** *(sharf)* . . . . scarf
❏ **Швеция** *(shvet-see-yah)* . . . . Sweden
❏ — where they speak **по-шведски** *(pah-shved-skee)*
❏ **штат** *(shtaht)* . . . . state
❏ **шторм** *(shtorm)* . . . . storm

Ш

What about inquiring about the price of **билетов?** *(beel-yet-tohv)* tickets **Вы можете** *(mohzh-yet-yeh)* can ask these **вопросы.**

(beel-yet)
Сколько стоит билет в Петербург? _____

(ah-des-soo)
Сколько стоит билет в Одессу? _____

(mahsk-voo)
Сколько стоит билет в Москву? _____

(ahd-nohm) *(nah-prahv-lyen-ee-ee)*
в одном направлении _____
one-way

(too-dah) *(ahb-raht-nah)*
туда и обратно _____
there and back, round trip

What about times of **отправления** *(aht-prahv-lyen-ee-yah)* departure **и прибытия?** *(pree-bit-ee-yah)* arrival **Вы тоже можете** *(toh-zheh)* ask these **вопросы.**

(kahg-dah) *(aht-hah-deet)* *(tahsh-kyent)*
Когда отходит поезд в Ташкент? _____
when departs Tashkent

(oo-lee-tah-yet) *(sah-mahl-yoht)*
Когда улетает самолёт в Москву? _____
flies away

(voh) *(vlah-dee-vah-stohk)*
Когда улетает самолёт во Владивосток? _____
to

(pree-hoh-deet) *(ree-gee)*
Когда приходит поезд из Риги? _____
arrives from Riga

(bah-koo)
Когда приходит поезд из Баку? _____
Baku

Вы have just arrived **в Россию. Вы теперь на вокзале.** at **Вы хотите ехать в Петербург?** *(vahk-zahl-yeh)* *(hah-teet-yeh)* want to go

(kee-yev)
или в Киев? Kiev **или в Москву? или в Одессу?** Tell that to the person at **окне** window selling **билеты.**

(ah-des-soo)
Я хочу поехать в Одессу. _____
Odessa

Когда отходит поезд в Одессу? _____

Сколько стоит билет в Одессу? _____

84

Теперь that **вы** know the words essential for traveling – be it throughout **Россия, Украина,** *(oo-krah-ee-nah)*
Ukraine

(toork-men-ee-stahn)
Туркменистан или *(kah-zahk-stahn)* **Казахстан** – what are some speciality items **вы** might go in search of?
Turkmenistan   Kazakstan

(mah-tryohsh-kah)
матрёшка
nesting dolls

(bah-lah-lie-kah)
балалайка
balalaika

(sah-mah-var)
самовар
samovar

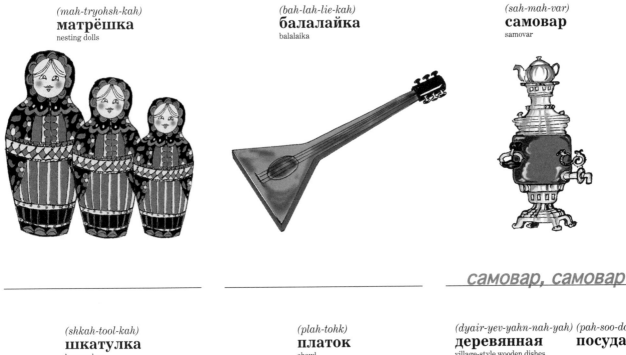

самовар, самовар

(shkah-tool-kah)
шкатулка
lacquer box

(plah-tohk)
платок
shawl

(dyair-yev-yahn-nah-yah) (pah-soo-dah)
деревянная   посуда
village-style wooden dishes

Consider using RUSSIAN *a language map*® as well. RUSSIAN *a language map*® is the perfect companion for your travels when **вы** may not wish to take along this book. Each section focuses on essentials for your trip. Your *Language Map*® is not meant to replace learning **русскии**, but will help you in the event **вы** forget something and need a little bit of help. For more information about the *Language Map*® Series, please turn to page 132 or go to www.bbks.com.

❑ **экватор** *(ek-vah-tar)* . . . . equator
❑ **экзамен** *(ek-zah-myen)* . . . . exam
❑ **экономика** *(ek-ah-noh-mee-kah)* . . . . economics   **э**
❑ **экспресс** *(ek-spres)* . . . . express
❑ **эра** *(air-ah)* . . . . era

Вы теперь в России и *(oo)* **у** *(vahs)* **вас есть номер. Вы** *(hah-teet-yeh)* **хотите** *(yest)* **есть. Где** *(hah-roh-shee)* **хороший** *(res-tah-rahn)* **ресторан?**
you have · you · are hungry · good

First of all, there are different types of places to eat. Let's learn them.

(res-tah-rahn)
ресторан _____

the most expensive of **русских** restaurants — frequently a dinner-and-dance establishment

(stah-loh-vah-yah)
столовая _____

generally self-service, similar to a cafeteria **или** canteen, and yes it also means "dining room"

(boo-fyet)
буфет _____

a snack bar generally found in **гостиницах**, theaters, **музеях**, bus **и** train stations

(bar)
бар _____

exactly that, a place, **где** drinks are served – this is where you come for Russian **водка!**

(kah-fyeh)
кафе _____

similar to a restaurant, meals are served thoughout the evening

If **вы** look around you **в русском ресторане, вы** will see that some **русские** customs might be different from ours. **Хлеб** *(hlyeb)* may be set directly on the tablecloth, elbows are often rested **на** *(nah)* **столе и** please **не** *(nyeh)* forget to mop up your **соус** *(soh-oos)* sauce **хлебом.** *(hlyeb-ahm)* with your bread Before beginning your **обед,** *(ah-byed)* be sure to wish those sharing your table – "**Приятного аппетита.**" *(pree-yaht-nah-vah)* *(ah-peh-tee-tah)* enjoy your meal Your turn to practice now.

_____
(enjoy your meal)

And at least one more time for practice!

_____
(enjoy your meal)

❏ **эскалатор** *(es-kah-lah-tor)* .... escalator
❏ **январь** *(yahn-var)*..................... January   **Э** _____
❏ **Япония** *(yah-pohn-ee-yah)* .... Japan
❏ —where they speak **по-японски** *(pah-yah-pohn-skee)*   **Я** _____
❏ **яхта** *(yahk-tah)* .... yacht

There are some **рестораны** whose names are indicative of the foods they serve.

Here you will find — *(shahsh-leek)* **шашлык** — *(pee-rahzh-kee)* **пирожки** — *(blee-nee)* **блины** — *(pyel-myen-ee)* **пельмени** — *(zah-koo-skee)* **закуски!**

shashlik, kebabs — pastries, small cakes — pancakes — pelmeni, dumplings — snacks

Try them all. Experiment. **Теперь вы** have found *(hah-roh-shee)* **хороший** *(res-tah-rahn)* **ресторан. Вы** *(vhah-deet-yeh)* **входите в** enter

(nah-hoh-deet-yeh) **ресторан и находите** *(myes-tah)* **место.** Sharing *(stoh-lih)* **столы с** others is a common **и** *(oh-chen)* **очень** pleasant

find — seat — tables

custom. If **вы** *(vee-deet-yeh)* **видите** a vacant *(stool)* **стул**, be sure to ask,

see — chair

Извините. Это место *(zahn-yah-tah)* **занято?** occupied

If **вам** *(vahm)* **нужно** *(noozh-nah)* **меню,** catch the attention of **официант,** *(ah-feet-see-ahnt)*

you need — waiter

Официант! *(die-tee)* **Дайте мне меню,** *(pah-zhahl-oos-tah)* **пожалуйста.**

(Waiter! Please, give me a menu.)

If your **официант** asks if **вы** enjoyed your **обед,** *(ah-byed)* a

smile **и** "**Да, спасибо,**" will tell him that **вы** did.

Most **русские рестораны** *(res-tah-rahn-ih)* post **меню** outside **или** inside. Do not hesitate to ask to see **меню**

before being seated so **вы знаете** *(znah-yet-yeh)* what type of **обеды** *(ah-byed-ih)* **и цены** *(tsyen-ih)* **вы** will encounter. Most

know — meals — prices

рестораны offer a special meal of the day. This is a complete **обед** *(ah-byed)* at a fair **цене.** *(tsyen-yeh)* Be

meal — price

forewarned that sometimes all items **в меню** are **не** available. Have a second choice in mind.

Вот a few special greetings **по-русски.**
- ❏ **С Рождеством Христовым!** *(suh)(rahzh-dyest-vohm)(hrees-toh-vim)* . . . . Merry Christmas!
- ❏ **С Новым годом!** *(suh)(noh-vim)(go-dahm)* . . . . Happy New Year!
- ❏ **С днём рождения!** *(suh)(den-yohm)(rahzh-dyen-ee-yah)* . . . . Happy Birthday!
- ❏ **Поздравления!** *(pahz-drahv-lyen-ee-yah)* . . . . Congratulations!

В России there are **три** main meals to enjoy every day, plus **кофе** *(koh-fyeh)* **и** perhaps pastry **для** *(dil-yah)* the
for

tired traveler late in **днём.** *(den-yohm)*
afternoon

завтрак *(zahv-trahk)* _____
breakfast

can mean much more than **чай или кофе, хлеб, масло и** jam. It may include ham **и яйца,** *(yight-sah)*

сыр или *(seer)* **сосиски.** *(sah-see-skee)* Check serving times before **вы** retire for the night or you might miss out!
cheese   small sausages

обед *(ah-byed)* _____
mid-day meal

generally served from 14:00 to 16:00. For most, this is the main meal of the day.

ужин *(oo-zheen)* _____
evening meal

generally served from 19:00 to 22:30; frequently, after 22:30, only cold items are served.

Most **рестораны** have a standard **меню.** Don't expect to get a separate wine list—it is usually

printed on **меню.** Service can be slow, so be prepared to wait between courses. **Теперь** for a

preview of delights to come . . . At the back of this **книги,** *(kuh-nee-gee)* **вы** will find a sample **русское**

меню. Read **меню сегодня** *(see-vohd-nyah)* **и** learn **новые слова! Когда вы** are ready to leave for **Россию**
today

cut out **меню,** fold it **и** carry it in your pocket, wallet **или** purse. Before you go, how do **вы** say

these **три** phrases which are so very important for the hungry traveler?

Excuse me. Is this seat occupied? _____

Waiter! Please, give me a menu. _____

Enjoy your meal! _____

_____ (who) **ест суп?** eats   _____ (who) **пьёт чай?** drinks

_____ (who) **путешествует в Одессу?**

(who)

Learning the following should help you to identify what kind of meat **вы** have ordered **и как** it will be prepared.
- ❒ **говядина** *(gahv-yah-dee-nah)* . . . . beef _____
- ❒ **телятина** *(tyel-yah-tee-nah)* . . . . veal _____
- ❒ **свинина** *(svee-nee-nah)* . . . . pork _____
- ❒ **баранина** *(bah-rah-nee-nah)* . . . . mutton

The **меню внизу** has the main categories **вы** will find in most restaurants. Learn them

(see-vohd-nyah)
сегодня   so that **вы** will easily recognize them when you dine **в России**. Be sure to write the
today

words in the blanks below.

(men-yoo)
Меню

(zah-koo-skee)
закуски
appetizers

(soop)
суп
soup

(yight-sah)
яйца
eggs

(rih-bah)
рыба
fish dishes

(myah-sah)
мясо
meat dishes

(pteet-sah)   *(deech)*
птица и **дичь**
poultry   and game

(oh-vahsh-chee)
овощи
vegetables

(sah-laht)
салат
salad

(dyes-yairt)
десерт
dessert

(slahd-kee-yeh) *(bloo-dah)*
сладкие блюда
sweets

(frook-tih)   *(seer)*
фрукты или сыр
fruit   cheese

(pee-rohzh-nee-yeh)
пирожные
pastries, small cakes

(nah-peet-kee)
напитки
beverages

❑ **домашняя птица** *(dah-mahsh-nyah-yah)(pteet-sah)* . . . . poultry _____
❑ **молодая баранина** *(mah-lah-dah-yah)(bah-rah-nee-nah)* . . . . . lamb _____
❑ **оленина** *(ahl-yeh-nee-nah)* . . . . venison _____
❑ **отварное** *(aht-var-noh-yeh)* . . . . boiled _____
❑ **жареное** *(zhar-yen-ah-yeh)* . . . . roasted, fried _____

Вы will also get **овощи** *(oh-vahsh-chee)* (vegetables) with your **обедом** *(ah-byed-ahm)* (meal) **и** perhaps **салат.** One day at an open-air **рынке** *(rin-kyeh)* (market) will teach you **названия** *(nahz-vah-nee-yah)* (names) for all the different kinds of **овощей и фруктов,** *(ah-vahsh-chay) (frook-tahv)* (fruit) plus it will be a delightful experience for you. **Вы можете** *(mohzh-yet-yeh)* always consult your menu guide at the back of **книги** *(kuh-nee-gee)* if **вы** forget the correct **название. Теперь вы** are seated **и официант** *(ah-feet-see-ahnt)* arrives.

Завтрак *(zahv-trahk)* (breakfast) can vary from a light continental breakfast to a hearty breakfast of eggs **или** cold cuts **или** vegetables. **Внизу** is a sample of what **вы можете** *(mohzh-yet-yeh)* expect to greet you **утром.** *(oo-trahm)* (in morning)

Напитки

чай с лимоном

кофе чёрный

кофе с молоком

апельсиновый сок
orange / juice

какао

Яйца

омлет с сыром
cheese

взбитая яичница
scrambled / eggs

И . . .

сыр
cheese

пирожные
pastry

булочки
rolls

масло

варенье
jam

Мясо

сосиски
small sausages, hot dogs

колбаса
sausage

❏ **тушёное** *(toosh-yoh-nah-yeh)* . . . . stewed
❏ **запечённое** *(zahp-yeh-chyohn-nah-yeh)* . . . . . baked
❏ **мясо-грилль** *(myah-sah-greel)* . . . . grilled
❏ **фаршированый** *(far-shee-roh-vah-nee)* . . . . . stuffed
❏ **фри** *(free)* . . . . fried

Вот an example of what **вы** might select for your evening meal. Using your menu guide on pages 117 and 118, as well as what **вы** have learned in this Step, fill in the blanks *in English* with what **вы** believe your **официант** will bring you. **Ответы внизу.**

Супы
Традиционный русский суп "Рыбная солянка"

_____

Салаты и закуски
Фрукты с йогуртом

_____

Основные блюда
Шашлык из баранины со сладким перцем, луком и рис "Шафран"

_____

Десерты
Десерт из бананов и мороженого

_____

(when) (how) (why)

Теперь it is a good time for a quick review. Draw lines between the *(roos-skee-mee) (slah-vah-mee)* **русскими словами и** their English equivalents.

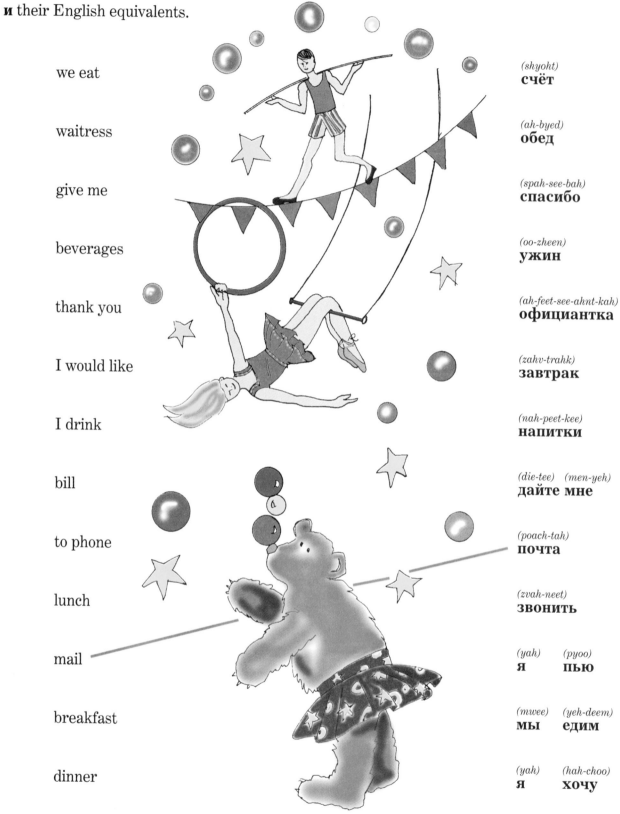

we eat	*(shyoht)* **счёт**
waitress	*(ah-byed)* **обед**
give me	*(spah-see-bah)* **спасибо**
beverages	*(oo-zheen)* **ужин**
thank you	*(ah-feet-see-ahnt-kah)* **официантка**
I would like	*(zahv-trahk)* **завтрак**
I drink	*(nah-peet-kee)* **напитки**
bill	*(die-tee) (men-yeh)* **дайте мне**
to phone	*(poach-tah)* **почта**
lunch	*(zvah-neet)* **звонить**
mail	*(yah) (pyoo)* **я пью**
breakfast	*(mwee) (yeh-deem)* **мы едим**
dinner	*(yah) (hah-choo)* **я хочу**

Вот a few more holidays which you might experience during your visit.
- ❑ **День победы** *(dyen)(pah-byeh-dee)* . . . . Victory Day
- ❑ **День независимости России** *(dyen)(nyeh-zah-vee-see-mah-stee)(rahs-see-ee)* . . Russian Independence Day
- ❑ **День Конституции** *(dyen)(kahn-stee-toot-see-ee)* . . . . Constitution Day
- ❑ **Праздник весны** *(prah-zneek)(vees-nee)* . . . . Spring Holiday

92

(teh-leh-fohn)
Телефон
telephone

What is different about *(teh-leh-fohn)* **телефон в России?** Well, **вы** never notice such things until **вы** want

to use them. Be warned **теперь** that *(teh-leh-fohn-ih)* **телефоны в России** are much less numerous than **в**

(seh-sheh-ah) **США или в Канаде.** Nevertheless, **телефон** allows you to call *(drooz-yahm)* **друзьям,** reserve *(beel-yet-ih)* **билеты**
friends

(tee-ah-ter) *(bahl-yet)* *(kahn-tsairt)* **в театр, на балет и концерт,** make emergency calls, check on the hours of a *(moo-zyeh-yah)* **музея,** rent

(mah-shee-noo) **машину и** all those other things which **нам нужно сделать** on a daily basis. It also gives
we need to do

you a certain amount of freedom, **когда вы можете позвонить** on your own.
phone

Having **телефон в номере гостиницы**

не as common **в России** as **в США.** That

means that **вам нужно знать, как** to
(vahm) (noozh-nah) (znaht)
to know

find **телефон: на почте, на улице, в**
(poach-teh) (oo-leet-seh)
street

баре и in the lobby of **гостиницы.**
(bar-yeh)

So, let's learn how to operate **телефон.**

Инструкции can look complicated,
(een-strook-tsee-ee)
instructions

but remember, some of these **слова**

вы should be able to recognize already.

Ready? Well, before you turn the page

it would be a good idea to go back **и**

review all your numbers one more time.

To dial from the United States to any other country **вы** need that country's international area

code. Your **телефонная книга** at home should have a listing of international area codes. When

Вот some **очень** useful words built around the word, "**телефон.**"
- ❏ **телефонист** *(teh-leh-fahn-eest)* . . . . operator _____
- ❏ **телефон-автомат** *(teh-leh-fohn-ahv-tah-maht)* . . . . public telephone booth _____
- ❏ **телефонная книга** *(teh-leh-fohn-nah-yah)(kuh-nee-gah)* . . telephone book _____
- ❏ **разговор по телефону** *(rahz-gah-vor)(pah)(teh-leh-foh-noo)* . telephone conversation _____

вы leave your contact numbers with friends, family или business colleagues, вы should include your destination country's area code и city code whenever possible. For example,

Country Codes		City Codes	
Russia	7	Moscow	095
		St. Petersburg	812
Ukraine	7	Kiev	044
		Odessa	0482
Lithuania	370	Kaunas	7

To call from one city to another city в России, you may need to go на почту *(poach-too)* или звонить телефонисту из гостиницы. На почте tell телефонисту "Мне нужно позвонить в США," или "Мне нужно позвонить в Англию."

operator

Now you try it: _____

(I need to call to the U.S.A.)

Do not be surprised if вы have to pay for your call in advance.

When answering телефон, вы pick up the receiver и say, *(ahl-loh)* Алло. Это _____ .

(your name)

When saying goodbye, you say "До свидания" or "До завтра." Your turn —

until   tomorrow

_____

(Hello. This is . . .)

_____   _____

(goodbye)   (until tomorrow)

Не forget that вы *(mohzh-yet-yeh)* можете ask . . .

can

Сколько стоит позвонить в **США?** *(seh-sheh-ah)* _____

U.S.A.

Сколько стоит позвонить в Англию? _____

Вот free telephone calls.
- ❏ **пожарная охрана** *(pah-zhar-nah-yah)(ah-hrah-nah)* . . . fire _____
- ❏ **милиция** *(mee-leet-see-yah)* . . . . police _____
- ❏ **скорая помощь** *(skoh-rah-yah)(poh-mashch)* . . . . emergency medical help _____
- ❏ **служба газа** *(sloozh-bah)(gah-zah)* . . . . heating gas service _____

(voht)
Вот some sample sentences **по** *(teh-leh-foh-noo)* **телефону.** Write them in the blanks **внизу.**

(hah-choo) *(chee-kah-goh)*
Я хочу позвонить в Чикаго. _____
to call   Chicago

(kahs-soo) *(ah-air-ah-floh-tah)* *(ah-air-ah-par-too)*
Я хочу позвонить в кассу "Аэрофлота" в аэропорту. _____
booking office of

(lohn-dahn)
Я хочу позвонить в Лондон. _____ *Я хочу позвонить в Лондон.* _____

(moy) *(nohm-yair)*
Мой номер 344-21-89. _____
my

(vahsh) *(pah-zhahl-oos-tah)*
Ваш номер телефона, пожалуйста? _____
your   number

(naht-see-oh-nahl)
Номер телефона гостиницы "Националь," пожалуйста? _____
hotel

(ee-vahn) *(ee-vah-nah-veech)* *(pah-gah-vah-reet)* *(ahn-noy)*
Иван: Алло. Это Иван Иванович. Я хочу поговорить с Анной Петровной.
to speak

_____

(syek-ryair-tar) *(noh)* *(lee-nee-yah)* *(zahn-yah-tah)*
Секретарь: Одну минуту. Извините, но линия занята.
one   but line   busy

_____

(pahv-tah-reet-yeh) *(myed-lyen-nah)*
Иван: Повторите, пожалуйста. Говорите медленно, пожалуйста.
repeat   speak   slowly

_____

Секретарь: Извините, но линия занята.

_____

Иван: Спасибо. До свидания.

_____

(myed-lyen-nah)
Вы теперь ready to use any **телефон в России.** Just take it **медленно** и speak clearly.
slowly

Вот countries, **где русский язык,** as well as other languages, is spoken that **вы** may wish to call.
- ❏ **Азербайджан** *(ah-zyair-by-dzhan)* . . . . Azerbaijan   _____
- ❏ **Армения** *(ar-myeh-nee-yah)* . . . . Armenia   _____
- ❏ **Беларусь** *(byeh-lah-roos)* . . . . Belarus   _____
- ❏ **Грузия** *(groo-zee-yah)* . . . . Georgia   _____

(myeh-troh)
Метро
subway

An excellent means of transportation **в России** is (myeh-troh) **метро.** In many cities, **метро** is an

extensive system with express lines to the suburbs. (trahm-vy) **Трамвай** is also a good means of
streetcar

transportation, plus **вы можете** see your surroundings (trahm-vah-yeh) **на трамвае.**

(myeh-troh)
метро
subway

(trahm-vy)
трамвай
streetcar, trolley

(stahnt-see-yah)
станция метро
station

(ahs-tah-nohv-kah) (trahm-vah-yah)
остановка трамвая
stop

(ahv-toh-boo-sah)
остановка автобуса
stop

Maps displaying the various (lee-nee-ee) **линии** и (ahs-tah-nohv-kee) **остановки** are generally posted inside (stahnt-see-ee) **станции**
lines stops

метро. Almost every **карта Москвы и Петербурга** has **метро** map. (lee-nee-ee) **Линии** are color-coded
lines

to facilitate reading just like your example on the next page. **Метро в Москве** is famous for its

elaborate stations with mosaics **и** sculptures. Enjoy them as **вы** pass through.

□ **Казахстан** *(kah-zahk-stahn)*. . . . . Kazakhstan _____
□ **Кыргызстан** *(kir-geez-stahn)*. . . . . Kyrgyzstan _____
□ **Латвия** *(laht-vee-yah)*. . . . . Latvia _____
□ **Литва** *(leet-vah)*. . . . . Lithuania _____
□ **Молдова** *(mahl-doh-vah)*. . . . . Moldova _____

Other than having foreign words, the Russian **метро** functions just like **метро в США, в Канаде или в Англии.** Locate your destination, select the correct line on your practice **метро и** hop on board.

Пл. Революции
Университет
Вокзал
Аэропорт
Библиотека
Зоопарк
ГУМ
Невский проспект
Большой театр
Проспект Мира
Арбатская
Центр
Театральная
Эрмитаж
Стадион
Пионерская
Гостиный двор
Академическая
Пушкинская
Парк культуры
Технологический институт

Say these questions aloud many times!

(stahnt-see-yah)
Где станция метро?

(ahs-tah-nohv-kah)
Где остановка автобуса?

(stah-yahn-kah)
Где стоянка такси?
taxi stand

(trahm-vah-yah)
Где остановка трамвая?

МОСКОВСКИЙ МЕТРОПОЛИТЕН

- ❏ **Таджикистан** *(tahd-zheek-ee-stahn)* . . . . Tajikistan
- ❏ **Туркменистан** *(toork-men-ee-stahn)* . . . . Turkmenistan
- ❏ **Украина** *(oo-krah-ee-nah)* . . . . Ukraine
- ❏ **Узбекистан** *(ooz-bek-ee-stahn)* . . . . Uzbekistan
- ❏ **Эстония** *(es-toh-nee-yah)* . . . . Estonia

Practice the following basic **вопросы** out loud **и** then write them in the blanks below.

1. *(chahs-tah) (hoh-deet)*
    Как часто ходит автобус номер 36? _____
    how often goes

    (trahm-vy)
    Как часто ходит трамвай номер 20? _____

2. *(ee-dyoht)*
    Идёт автобус до Большого театра? _____
    goes

    Идёт трамвай до зоопарка? _____

    Идёт поезд до гостиницы "Метрополь"? _____

3. **Сколько стоит билет в метро?** _____ *Сколько стоит билет в метро?*

    Сколько стоит билет в автобусе? _____

    Сколько стоит билет на поезд? _____

    Сколько стоит билет в трамвае? _____

4. *(mah-goo)*
    Где я могу купить билет на метро? _____
    can buy

    Где я могу купить билет на автобус? _____

    Где я могу купить билет на поезд? _____

Let's change directions **и** learn **три** new verbs. **Вы** know the basic "plug-in" formula, so write

out your own sentences using these new verbs.

(stee-raht)
стирать _____
to wash (clothes)

(tyair-yaht)
терять _____
to lose

(zah-nee-mah-yet)
занимает _____
it takes

Вот a few holidays to keep in mind.
- ❐ **Пасха** *(pahs-hkah)* . . . . Easter
- ❐ **Новый год** *(noh-vee)(gohd)* . . . . New Year's Day
- ❐ **Рождество** *(rahsh-dyest-voh)* . . . . Russian Orthodox Christmas
- ❐ **Международный женский день** *(myezh-doo-nah-rohd-nee)(zhen-skee)(dyen)* . . International Women's Day

(prah-dah-vaht)   *(pah-koo-paht)*

Продавать и покупать
to sell   to buy

Shopping abroad is exciting. The simple everyday task of buying **литр молока или яблоко**

(lee-ter)   *(mah-lah-kah)*   *(yah-blah-kah)*
     liter   milk   apple

becomes a challenge that **вы** should **теперь** be able to meet quickly **и** easily. Of course, **вы** will

purchase **сувениры, марки и открытки,** but **не** forget those many other items ranging from

(soo-veh-neer-ih)
souvenirs

shoelaces to **аспирина** that **вы** might need unexpectedly. Locate your store, draw a line to it **и,**

(ah-spee-ree-nah)
aspirin

as always, write your new words in the blanks provided.

(oo-nee-vyair-mahg)
универмаг _____
department store

(kee-noh)
кино _____
cinema

(poach-tah)
почта _____
post office

(bahnk)
банк _____
bank

(gah-stee-neet-sah)
гостиница _____
hotel, inn

(byen-zah-kah-lohn-kah)
бензоколонка _____
service station

(mah-gah-zeen-ih) **Магазины** are generally **открыты** from *(aht-krih-tih)*
open

8:00 or 10:00 until 19:00 or 20:00. Keep in

mind, many shops close over the lunch hour.

(myahs-noy) **мясной** *(mah-gah-zeen)* **магазин** *(kuh-nee-gee)* **книги**
butcher   shop   bookstore

_____   _____

(heem-cheest-kah)
_____ **химчистка**
dry cleaners

(oh-vahsh-chee)
_____ **овощи**
greengrocer

(ahp-tyek-ah)
_____ **аптека**
pharmacy

(stah-yahn-kah)
_____ **стоянка**
parking lot

(kee-ohsk)
_____ **киоск**
newsstand

(gah-strah-nohm)
_____ **гастроном**
grocery store, delicatessen

(tah-bahk)
_____ **табак**
tobacco

While **в Москве вы** will want to visit **ГУМ**, short for "**Государственный** *(gah-soo-darst-vyen-nee)* **универсальный** *(oo-nee-vyair-sahl-nee)*

магазин." **ГУМ** sells everything!

(byoo-roh) **бюро** *(poot-yeh-shest-vee-ee)* **путешествий** *(mee-leet-see-yah)* **милиция**
travel agency   police

_____   _____

(mah-lah-koh)
молоко
dairy

_____

(tsvet-ih)
цветы
flowers

_____

(rib-nee)   *(rin-ahk)*
рыбный рынок _____
fish market

(foh-tah-tah-vah-rih)
фототовары _____
camera supplies

(rin-ahk)
рынок _____
market

(prahd-mahg)
продмаг _____
food store

(chah-sih)
часы _____
watchmaker

(boo-lahch-nah-yah)
булочная   *булочная, булочная*
bakery

(kah-fyeh)
кафе _____
cafe

(prahch-yech-nah-yah)
прачечная _____
laundry

(kahnt-stah-vah-rih)
канцтовары
stationery store

_____

(pah-reek-mahk-yairs-kah-yah)
парикмахерская
hairdresser

_____

While **Москва** has **ГУМ**, *(goom)* **Санкт-Петербург**

has "**Гостиный** *(gah-stee-nee)* **двор.**" *(dvor)* **Гостиный двор**

is the city's largest shopping mall. Enjoy

shopping, browsing or just people-watching.

At this point, **вы** should just about be ready for your **поездки**. **Вы** have gone shopping for those last-minute odds 'n ends. Most likely, the store directory at your local **универсальный магазин** *(oo-nee-vyair-sahl-nee)* did not look like the one **внизу**. **Вы знаете**, that *(zhen-shchee-nah)* "**женщина**" is Russian for "<u>woman</u>" so if **вам нужно** something for a woman, **вы** would probably look **на втором этаже,** *(vtah-rohm)* second *(eh-tahzh-yeh)* floor wouldn't you?

5. этаж	Хрусталь Фарфор Керамика Товары для кухни	Кафе Вино Фрукты Овощи	Мороженое Булочная Спиртные напитки Ресторан
4. этаж	Кровати Постельное Бельё Зеркала Мебель	Лампы Ковры Картины Электроприборы	Телевизоры Фототовары Радио
3. этаж	Детский отдел Детская обувь Купальные костюмы	Спортивные товары Кожаные товары Перчатки	Принадлежности туалета Ювелирные изделия Часы
2. этаж	Женская одежда Женские головные уборы Женская обувь	Мужская одежда Мужские головные уборы Мужская обувь	Носки, чулки Пояса Зонты
1. этаж	Книги Табак Газеты Журналы	Карты Конфеты Игрушки Духи	Косметика Музыкальные товары Канцтовары

Let's start a checklist **для поездки**. Besides **одежды, что вам нужно?** *(ah-dyezh-dih)* clothes As you learn these **слова,** assemble these items **в углу** of your **дома**. Check **и** make sure that **они** are clean **и** corner ready **для поездки**. *(pah-yezd-kee)* trip Be sure to do the same **с** the rest of **вещами** *(vesh-chah-mee)* things that **вы** pack. On the next pages, match each item to its picture, draw a line to it and write out the word many times. As **вы** organize these things, check them off on this list. Do not forget to take the next group of

sticky labels and label **эти вещи сегодня.** *(et-tee)* *(see-vohd-nyah)*

(pahs-part)
паспорт
passport

_____ ☐

(beel-yet)
билет
ticket

_____ ☐

(cheh-mah-dahn)
чемодан
suitcase

_____ ☐

(soom-kah)
сумка
handbag

сумка, сумка, сумка _____ ☑

(boo-mahzh-neek)
бумажник
wallet

_____ ☐

(dyen-gee)
деньги
money

_____ ☐

(kreh-deet-nah-yah) *(kar-tahch-kah)*
кредитная карточка
credit   card

_____ ☐

(dah-rohzh-nih-yeh) *(cheh-kee)*
дорожные чеки
traveler's   checks

_____ ☐

(foh-tah-ahp-pah-raht)
фотоаппарат
camera

_____ ☐

(foh-tah-plyohn-kah)
фотоплёнка
film

(koo-pahl-nee) *(kahst-yoom)*
купальный костюм
swimsuit

_____ ☐

(koo-pahl-nee) *(kahst-yoom)*
купальный костюм
swimsuit

_____ ☐

(sahn-dahl-ee-ee)
сандалии
sandals

_____ ☐

(tyohm-nih-yeh) *(ahch-kee)*
тёмные очки
sunglasses

_____ ☐

(zoob-nah-yah) *(shchoht-kah)*
зубная щётка
toothbrush

_____ ☐

(zoob-nah-yah) *(pahs-tah)*
зубная паста
toothpaste

_____ ☐

(mwee-lah)
мыло
soap

_____ ☐

(breet-vah)
бритва
razor

_____ ☐

(dyeh-zah-dah-rahnt)
дезодорант
deodorant

_____ ☐

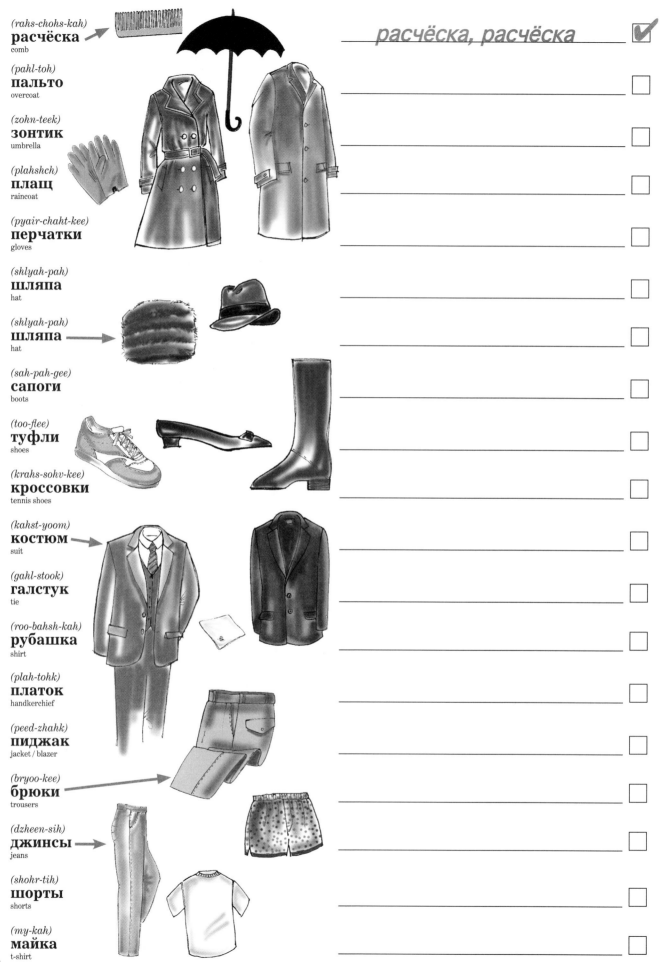

(rahs-chohs-kah)
расчёска
comb

(pahl-toh)
пальто
overcoat

(zohn-teek)
зонтик
umbrella

(plahshch)
плащ
raincoat

(pyair-chaht-kee)
перчатки
gloves

(shlyah-pah)
шляпа
hat

(shlyah-pah)
шляпа
hat

(sah-pah-gee)
сапоги
boots

(too-flee)
туфли
shoes

(krahs-sohv-kee)
кроссовки
tennis shoes

(kahst-yoom)
костюм
suit

(gahl-stook)
галстук
tie

(roo-bahsh-kah)
рубашка
shirt

(plah-tohk)
платок
handkerchief

(peed-zhahk)
пиджак
jacket / blazer

(bryoo-kee)
брюки
trousers

(dzheen-sih)
джинсы
jeans

(shohr-tih)
шорты
shorts

(my-kah)
майка
t-shirt

расчёска, расчёска

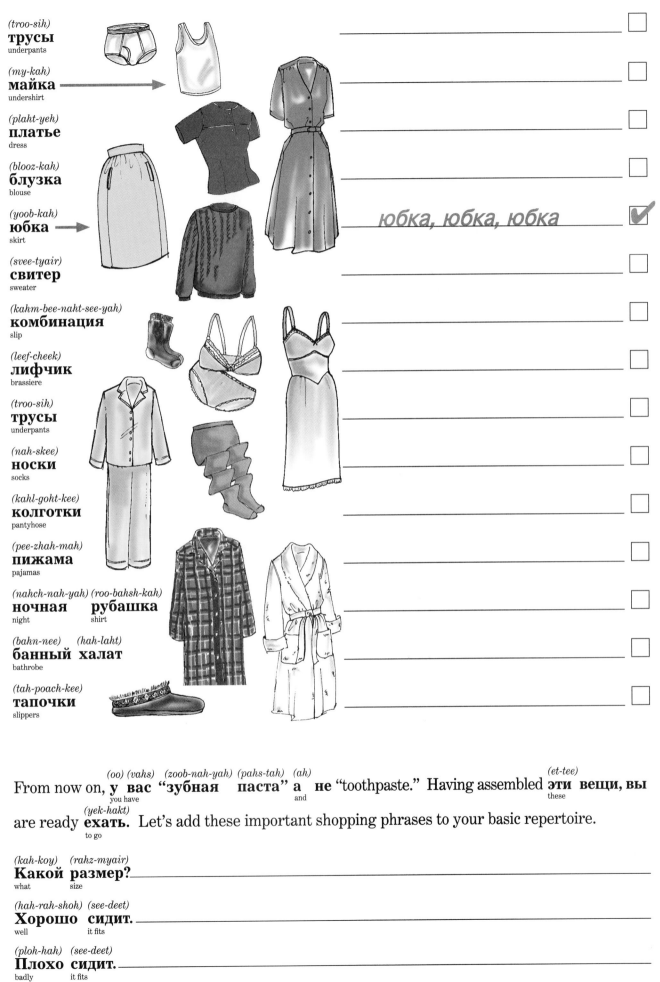

(troo-sih)
трусы
underpants

(my-kah)
майка
undershirt

(plaht-yeh)
платье
dress

(blooz-kah)
блузка
blouse

(yoob-kah)
юбка
skirt

юбка, юбка, юбка ✓

(svee-tyair)
свитер
sweater

(kahm-bee-naht-see-yah)
комбинация
slip

(leef-cheek)
лифчик
brassiere

(troo-sih)
трусы
underpants

(nah-skee)
носки
socks

(kahl-goht-kee)
колготки
pantyhose

(pee-zhah-mah)
пижама
pajamas

(nahch-nah-yah) (roo-bahsh-kah)
ночная   рубашка
night   shirt

(bahn-nee)   (hah-laht)
банный халат
bathrobe

(tah-poach-kee)
тапочки
slippers

(oo) (vahs) (zoob-nah-yah) (pahs-tah) (ah)   *(et-tee)*
From now on, **у вас** "**зубная   паста**" **а не** "toothpaste." Having assembled **эти вещи, вы**
 you have and these

 *(yek-hakt)*
are ready **ехать.** Let's add these important shopping phrases to your basic repertoire.
 to go

(kah-koy) (rahz-myair)
Какой размер?_____
what size

(hah-rah-shoh) (see-deet)
Хорошо сидит._____
well it fits

(ploh-hah) (see-deet)
Плохо сидит._____
badly it fits

105

Treat yourself to a final review. **Вы знаете** the names for **русских** **магазинов,** *(mah-gah-zee-nahv)* so let's practice

shopping. Just remember your basic **вопросы** that you learned in Step 2. Whether **вы** need to

buy **женские** **брюки** *(zhen-skee-yeh)* *(bryoo-kee)* **или книги** the necessary **слова** are the same.

1.   First step — **Где?**

Где кино?   **Где молоко?**   **Где банк?**   **Где** **булочная?** *(boo-lahch-nah-yah)*   **Где кафе?**

_____
(Where is the department store?)

_____
(Where is the grocery store / delicatessen?)

_____
(Where is the market?)

2.   Second step — tell them what **вы** are looking for, need **или хотите!**

Мне **нужно . . .** *(men-yeh)* *(noozh-nah)*
I   need

Я **хочу . . .** *(yah)* *(hah-choo)*
I   would like

У **вас есть . . . ?** *(oo)* *(vahs)* *(yest)*
do you have

_____
(Do you have postcards?)

_____
(I would like four stamps.)

_____
(I need toothpaste.)

_____
(I would like to buy film.)

_____
(Do you have coffee?)

Go through the glossary at the end of *(et-toy)* **этой книги и** select *(dvahd-tset)* **двадцать слов.** Drill the above
this

patterns **с** *(et-tee-mee)* **этими** twenty **словами.** Don't cheat. Drill them *(see-vohd-nyah)* **сегодня.** **Теперь** take
these

(dvahd-tset)
двадцать more **слов из** your glossary **и** do the same.

3.　　Third step — find out *(skohl-kah)* **сколько** *(et-tah)* **это** *(stoy-eet)* **стоит.**

(aht-krit-kah)	*(kee-loh)* *(yah-blahk)*
Сколько стоит марка?　　**Сколько стоит открытка?**　　**Сколько стоит кило яблок?**	
	kilo　　apples

_____

(How much does the toothpaste cost?)

_____

(How much does the soap cost?)

_____

(How much does a cup of tea cost?)

4.　　Fourth step — success! I found it!

Once **вы** find what **вы** would like, *(gah-vah-reet-yeh)* **говорите,**
say

Я хочу это, пожалуйста. _____

or

Дайте мне это, пожалуйста. _Дайте мне это, пожалуйста._

Или if **вы** would not like it

(et-tah-vah)
Я не хочу этого, спасибо. _____
that

or

(nah-dah)
Спасибо, не надо. _____
(it is) not right

Congratulations! You have finished. By now you should have stuck your labels, flashed your

cards, cut out your menu guide, and packed your suitcases. You should be very pleased with

your accomplishment. You have learned what it sometimes takes others years to achieve and

you hopefully had fun doing it. **Счастливого пути!**

Glossary

This glossary contains words used in this book only. It is not meant to be a dictionary. Consider purchasing a dictionary which best suits your needs—small for traveling, large for reference, or specialized for specific vocabulary needs.

The words here are all presented in **Russian** alphabetical order followed by the pronunciation guide used in this book. Remember that Russian words change their endings depending upon how they are used. Not all variations of a word will be given. Learn to look for the core of the word.

А

а *(ah)* .... but, and
абрикос *(ah-bree-kohs)* .... apricot
август *(ahv-goost)* .... August
авиа *(ah-vee-ah)* .... airmail
авиапочта *(ah-vee-ah-poach-tah)* .... by airmail
авиация *(ah-vee-aht-see-yah)* .... aviation
Австралия *(ahv-strah-lee-yah)* .... Australia
Австрия *(ahv-stree-yah)* .... Austria
автобиография *(ahv-tah-bee-ah-grah-fee-yah)* .... autobiography
автобус *(ahv-toh-boos)* .... bus
автобусы *(ahv-toh-boo-sih)* .... buses
автограф *(ahv-toh-grahf)* .... autograph
автомат *(ahv-tah-maht)* .... automat
автомобиль *(ahv-tah-mah-beel)* .... automobile, car
автор *(ahv-tar)* .... author
автостанция *(ahv-tah-stahnt-see-yah)* ..... service station
агент *(ah-gyent)* .... agent
адвокат *(ahd-vah-kaht)* .... advocate, lawyer
адрес *(ah-dres)* .... address
Азербайджан *(ah-zyair-by-dzhahn)* .... Azerbaijan
азербайджанец *(ah-zyair-by-dzhah-nyets)* .... Azerbaijanian
Азия *(ah-zee-yah)* .... Asia
академия *(ah-kah-dyeh-mee-yah)* .... academy
аккуратный *(ahk-koo-raht-nee)* ...... accurate, fastidious, neat
акробат *(ah-krah-baht)* .... acrobat
акт *(ahkt)* .... act
актёр *(ahk-tyor)* .... actor
акцент *(ahkt-syent)* .... accent
алгебра *(ahl-gyeh-brah)* .... algebra
алкоголь *(ahl-kah-gohl)* .... alcoholic drinks, alcohol
алло *(ahl-loh)* .... hello
алфавит *(ahl-fah-veet)* .... alphabet
Америка *(ah-myeh-ree-kah)* .... America
Америке *(ah-myeh-ree-kyeh)* .... America
Америку *(ah-myeh-ree-koo)* .... America
американец *(ah-myeh-ree-kah-nyets)* .... American male
американка *(ah-myeh-ree-kahn-kah)* ...... American female
Англия *(ahn-glee-yah)* .... England
Англию *(ahn-glee-yoo)* .... England
английский *(ahn-glee-skee)* .... English
англичанин *(ahn-glee-chah-neen)* .... Englishman
англичанка *(ahn-glee-chahn-kah)* .... Englishwoman
анекдот *(ah-nyek-doht)* .... anecdote, joke
антенна *(ahn-tyen-nah)* .... antenna
антибиотики *(ahn-tee-bee-oh-tee-kee)* ...... antibiotics
аппетит *(ah-peh-teet)* .... appetite
апрель *(ahp-ryel)* .... April
аптека *(ahp-tyek-ah)* .... pharmacy, drugstore
арена *(ar-yen-ah)* .... arena
арест *(ar-yest)* .... arrest
Армения *(ar-myeh-nee-yah)* .... Armenia
армянин *(ar-myah-neen)* .... Armenian
армия *(ar-mee-yah)* .... army
аспирин *(ah-spee-reen)* .... aspirin
астронавт *(ah-strah-nahvt)* .... astronaut
атлет *(aht-lyet)* .... athlete
Африка *(ah-free-kah)* .... Africa
аэродром *(ah-air-ah-drohm)* .... airfield
аэропорт *(ah-air-ah-port)* .... airport

Б

бабушка *(bah-boosh-kah)* .... grandmother
багаж *(bah-gahzh)* .... baggage
базар *(bah-zar)* .... bazaar
Баку *(bah-koo)* .... Baku

бал *(bahl)* .... ball (dance)
балалайка *(bah-lah-lie-kah)* .... balalaika
балерина *(bah-leh-ree-nah)* .... ballerina
банан *(bah-nahn)* .... banana
бандит *(bahn-deet)* .... bandit, robber
банк *(bahnk)* .... bank
банный халат *(bahn-nee)(hah-laht)* .... bathrobe
бар *(bar)* .... bar (restaurant)
баранина *(bah-rah-nee-nah)* .... mutton
баржа *(bar-zhah)* .... barge
барьер *(bar-yair)* .... barrier
бас *(bahs)* .... bass (voice)
баскетбол *(bah-sket-bohl)* .... basketball
батальон *(bah-tahl-yohn)* .... battalion
батарея *(bah-tar-yeh-yah)* .... battery
беден *(byed-yen)* .... poor
без *(byez)* .... minus, without
Беларусь *(byeh-lah-roos)* .... Belarus
беларус *(byeh-lah-roos)* .... Belarussian
белый *(byeh-lee)* .... white
Бельгия *(byel-gee-yah)* .... Belgium
бензоколонка *(byen-zah-kah-lohn-kah)* ... sevice station, gas pump
библиотека *(bee-blee-ah-tyeh-kah)* .... library
Библия *(bee-blee-yah)* .... Bible
билет *(beel-yet)* .... ticket
билеты *(beel-yet-ih)* .... tickets
бинокль *(bee-noh-kil)* .... binoculars
бланк *(blahnk)* .... blank (form)
блузка *(blooz-kah)* .... blouse
блюда *(bloo-dah)* .... dishes (food)
богат *(bah-gaht)* .... rich
бокал *(bah-kahl)* .... wine glass, glass
бокс *(bohks)* .... boxing
Болгария *(bahl-gar-ee-yah)* .... Bulgaria
болен *(bohl-yen)* .... sick
Боливия *(bah-lee-vee-yah)* .... Bolivia
больше *(bohl-shee)* .... more
большой *(bahl-shoy)* .... big, large
Большой театр *(bahl-shoy)(tee-ah-ter)* ... Bolshoi Theater
бомба *(bohm-bah)* .... bomb
борщ *(borshch)* .... borsch (beet soup)
брат *(braht)* .... brother
бритва *(breet-vah)* .... razor
бронза *(brohn-zah)* .... bronze
брюки *(bryoo-kee)* .... trousers
брюнет *(broo-nyet)* .... brunette (male)
будете пить *(boo-dyet-yeh)(peet)* ...... (you) will drink
будильник *(boo-deel-neek)* .... alarm clock
булочки *(boo-lahch-kee)* .... rolls
булочная *(boo-lahch-nah-yah)* .... bakery
бульвар *(bool-var)* .... boulevard
бумага *(boo-mah-gah)* .... paper
бумажник *(boo-mahzh-neek)* .... wallet
буфет *(boo-fyet)* .... snack bar, snack car
было *(bih-lah)* .... was
быстро *(bis-trah)* .... fast
бюро *(byoo-roh)* .... bureau, office
бюро проката *(byoo-roh)(prah-kah-tah)* ...... resntal agency
бюро путешествий *(byoo-roh)(poot-yeh-shest-vee-ee)* ... travel agency
бюрократ *(byoo-rah-kraht)* .... bureaucrat

В

в *(vuh)* .... at, in, on, to
в августе *(vuh)(ahv-goost-yeh)* .... in August
в апреле *(vuh)(ahp-ryel-yeh)* .... in April
в декабре *(vuh)(dee-kah-bryeh)* .... in December
в июле *(vuh)(ee-yool-yeh)* .... in July

в июне *(vuh)(ee-yoon-yeh)* . . . . in June
в мае *(vuh)(mah-yeh)* . . . . in May
в марте *(vuh)(mart-yeh)* . . . . in March
в ноябре *(vuh)(nah-yah-bryeh)* . . . . in November
в одном направлении *(vuh)(ahd-nohm)(nah-prahv-lyen-ee-ee)* . . . .
. . . . one-way
в октябре *(vuh)(ahk-tyah-bryeh)* . . . . in October
в сентябре *(vuh)(syen-tyah-bryeh)* . . . . in September
в феврале *(vuh)(fyev-rahl-yeh)* . . . . in February
в январе *(vuh)(yahn-var-yeh)* . . . . in January
вагон *(vah-gohn)* . . . . compartment, wagon
вагон-ресторан *(vah-gohn-res-tah-rahn)* . . dining compartment
важно *(vahzh-nah)* . . . . important
ваза *(vah-zah)* . . . . vase
вальс *(vahls)* . . . . waltz
вам *(vahm)* . . . . to you
вам нужно *(vahm)(noosh-nah)* . . . . you need
ванная *(vahn-nah-yah)* . . . . bathroom
ванной *(vahn-noy)* . . . . bathroom
ванную *(vahn-noo-yoo)* . . . . bathroom
варенье *(var-yen-yeh)* . . . . jam (food)
вас *(vahs)* . . . . you
вас зовут *(vahs)(zah-voot)* . . . . your name is
Ватикан *(vah-tee-kahn)* . . . . Vatican
ваш *(vahsh)* . . . . your
велосипед *(vyeh-lah-see-pyed)* . . . . bicycle
веранда *(vee-rahn-dah)* . . . . veranda
весной *(vees-noy)* . . . . in spring
ветрено *(vyet-ren-ah)* . . . . windy
вечер *(vyeh-cher)* . . . . evening
вещи *(vesh-chee)* . . . . things
видеть *(vee-dyet)* . . . . to see
виза *(vee-zah)* . . . . visa
вилка *(veel-kah)* . . . . fork
вино *(vee-noh)* . . . . wine
витамин *(vee-tah-meen)* . . . . vitamin
Владивосток *(vlah-dee-vah-stohk)* . . . . . . Vladivostok
внизу *(vnee-zoo)* . . . . downstairs, below
во *(voh)* . . . . to
вода *(vah-dah)* . . . . water
воды *(vah-dih)* . . . . water
водка *(vohd-kah)* . . . . vodka
вокзал *(vahk-zahl)* . . . . train station
Волга *(vohl-gah)* . . . . Volga River
волейбол *(vah-lay-bohl)* . . . . volleyball
вопрос *(vah-prohs)* . . . . question
вопросы *(vah-proh-sih)* . . . . questions
восемь *(voh-syem)* . . . . eight
восемнадцать *(vah-sim-nahd-tset)* . . . . eighteen
восемьдесят *(voh-syem-dyes-yet)* . . . . eighty
воскресенье *(vah-skree-syen-yeh)* . . . . Sunday
восток *(vah-stohk)* . . . . east
вот *(voht)* . . . . here is, here are
врач *(vrahch)* . . . . doctor
всё *(vsyoh)* . . . . everything
вторник *(vtor-neek)* . . . . Tuesday
втором этаж *(vtah-rohm)(eh-tahzh-yeh)* . . . second floor
вход *(vhohd)* . . . . entrance
входить *(vhah-deet)* . . . . to enter
вчера *(vchee-rah)* . . . . yesterday
въезд запрещён *(vyezd)(zah-presh-chyohn)* . . no entrance
вы *(vwee)* . . . . you
высокая *(vwee-soh-kah-yah)* . . . . high, tall
выход *(vwee-hahd)* . . . . exit
выходить *(vwee-hah-deet)* . . . . to go out, to exit

Г

газ *(gahz)* . . . . natural gas
газета *(gah-zyeh-tah)* . . . . gazette, newspaper
газету *(gah-zyeh-too)* . . . . newspaper
газетчик *(gah-zyet-cheek)* . . . . newspaper man
галерея *(gahl-yair-eh-yah)* . . . . gallery
галстук *(gahl-stook)* . . . . tie
гараж *(gah-rahzh)* . . . . garage
гастроном *(gah-strah-nohm)* . . . delicatessen, grocery store
где *(gdyeh)* . . . . where
генерал *(gee-nee-rahl)* . . . . general
география *(gee-ah-grah-fee-yah)* . . . . geography
геолог *(gee-oh-lahg)* . . . . geologist
геология *(gee-ah-loh-gee-yah)* . . . . geology

геометрия *(gee-ah-myet-ree-yah)* . . . . geometry
Гибралтар *(gee-brahl-tar)* . . . . Gibraltar
гид *(geed)* . . . . guide
гимнастика *(geem-nah-stee-kah)* . . . . gymnastics
гитара *(gee-tah-rah)* . . . . guitar
главная дорога *(glahv-nah-yah)(dah-roh-gah)* . . . . . right of way
главный вход *(glahv-nee)(vhohd)* . . . . . . main entrance
говорить *(gah-vah-reet)* . . . . to speak, to say
говядина *(gahv-yah-dee-nah)* . . . . beef
год *(gohd)* . . . . year
года *(go-dah)* . . . . year
году *(gah-doo)* . . . . year
голубой *(gah-loo-boy)* . . . . light blue
города *(go-rah-dah)* . . . . city
городами *(gah-rah-dah-mee)* . . . . cities
горячая *(gar-yah-chah-yah)* . . . . hot
гостиная *(gah-stee-nah-yah)* . . . . living room
гостиница *(gah-stee-neet-sah)* . . . . hotel, inn
гостинице *(gah-stee-neet-seh)* . . . . hotel, inn
Гостиный двор *(gah-stee-nee)(dvor)* . . . . .
. . . . department store in St. Petersburg
градусы *(grah-doo-sih)* . . . . degrees
грамм *(grahm)* . . . . gram
гранит *(grah-neet)* . . . . granite
Греция *(gret-see-yah)* . . . . Greece
Грузия *(groo-zee-yah)* . . . . Georgia
грузин *(groo-zeen)* . . . . Georgian
группа *(groop-pah)* . . . . group
ГУМ *(goom)* . . . . department store in Moscow
гусь *(goose)* . . . . goose

Д

да *(dah)* . . . . yes
дайте *(die-tee)* . . . . give!
дайте мне *(die-tee)(men-yeh)* . . . . give me
дама *(dah-mah)* . . . . dame, lady, woman
Дания *(dah-nee-yah)* . . . . Denmark
дата *(dah-tah)* . . . . date
два, две *(dvah),(dveh)* . . . . two
двадцать *(dvahd-tset)* . . . . twenty
двенадцать *(dveh-nahd-tset)* . . . . twelve
дверь *(dvyair)* . . . . door
движение запрещено *(dvee-zhen-ee-yeh)(zah-presh-chen-oh)* . . . . .
. . . . road closed to vehicles
девять *(dyev-yet)* . . . . nine
девяносто *(dyev-yah-noh-stah)* . . . . ninety
девятнадцать *(div-yet-nahd-tset)* . . . . nineteen
дедушка *(dyeh-doosh-kah)* . . . . grandfather
дедушку *(dyeh-doosh-koo)* . . . . grandfather
дезодорант *(dyeh-zah-dah-rahnt)* . . . . . . deodorant
декабрь *(dee-kah-bair)* . . . . December
делать *(dyeh-laht)* . . . . to do, to make
делать пересадку *(dyeh-laht)(pyair-yeh-sahd-koo)* . . . . . to transfer
делегат *(dyeh-leh-gaht)* . . . . delegate
демонстрация *(dyeh-mahn-straht-see-yah)* . . . . demonstration
день *(dyen)* . . . . day, afternoon
деньги *(dyen-gee)* . . . . money
денег *(dyen-yeg)* . . . . money
деревянная посуда *(dyair-yev-yahn-nah-yah)(pah-soo-dah)* . . . . .
. . . . village-style wooden dishes
десерт *(dyes-yairt)* . . . . dessert
десять *(dyes-yet)* . . . . ten
дети *(dyeh-tee)* . . . . children
детская обувь *(dyet-skah-yah)(oh-boov)* . . . children's footware
детский отдел *(dyet-skee)(aht-dyel)* . . . children's department
дешёвая *(dyeh-shyoh-vah-yah)* . . . . inexpensive
джаз *(dzhahz)* . . . . jazz
джин *(dzheen)* . . . . gin
джинсы *(dzheen-sih)* . . . . jeans
диагноз *(dee-ahg-nahz)* . . . . diagnosis
диаграмма *(dee-ah-grahm-mah)* . . . . diagram, blueprint
диалог *(dee-ah-lohg)* . . . . dialogue, conversation
диалоги *(dee-ah-loh-gee)* . . . . . dialogues, conversations
диван *(dee-vahn)* . . . . divan, sofa
дизель *(dee-zyel)* . . . . diesel
диплом *(dee-plohm)* . . . . diploma
дипломат *(dee-plah-maht)* . . . . diplomat
директор *(dee-rek-tar)* . . . . director
дискуссия *(dee-skoos-see-yah)* . . . . discussion
дичь *(deech)* . . . . game (food)

длинная *(dleen-nah-yah)* .... long
для *(dil-yah)* .... for
днём *(den-yohm)* .... afternoon
дня *(den-yah)* .... day
дни *(dnee)* .... days
дней *(dnay)* .... days
до *(doh)* .... to, until
до завтра *(dah)(zahv-trah)* .... until tomorrow
до свидания *(dah)(svee-dahn-ee-yah)* .... goodbye
доброе утро *(doh-brah-yeh)(oo-trah)* .... good morning
добрый вечер *(doh-brih)(vyeh-cher)* .... good evening
добрый день *(doh-brih)(dyen)* .... good day, good afternoon
дождь *(dohzhd)* .... rain
доктор *(dohk-tar)* .... doctor
документ *(dah-koo-myent)* .... document
доллар *(dohl-lar)* .... dollar
дом *(dohm)* .... house
дома *(doh-mah)* .... house
доме *(doh-myeh)* .... house
домашняя птица *(dah-mahsh-nyah-yah)(pteet-sah)* .... poultry
дорога *(dah-roh-gah)* .... road
дорогая *(dah-rah-gah-yah)* .... expensive
дорогу *(dah-roh-goo)* .... directions
дорожные чеки *(dah-rohzh-nih-yeh)(cheh-kee)*... traveler's checks
дочь *(dohch)* .... daughter
драма *(drah-mah)* .... drama
друзьям *(drooz-yahm)* .... friends
духи *(doo-hkee)* .... perfume
душ *(doosh)* .... shower
дядя *(dyah-dyah)* .... uncle

Е

еврей *(yev-ray)* .... Jewish man
еврейка *(yev-ray-kah)* .... Jewish woman
его зовут *(yee-voh)(zah-voot)* .... his name is
её зовут *(yee-yoh)(zah-voot)* .... her name is
емейл *(eh-mail)* .... email
есть *(yest)* .... to eat
ехать *(yek-haht)* ..... to go, to ride (with a means of transportation)
ехать на машине *(yek-haht)(nah)(mah-shee-nyeh)* ...... to drive

Ж

жакет *(zhah-kyet)* .... jacket
жареное *(zhar-yen-ah-yeh)* .... roasted, fried
жарко *(zhar-kah)* .... hot
жасмин *(zhahs-meen)* .... jasmine
ждать *(zhdaht)* .... to wait for
желе *(zhel-yeh)* .... jelly
женский *(zhen-skee)* .... ladies' (restroom)
женщина *(zhen-shchee-nah)* .... woman
женская обувь *(zhen-skah-yah)(oh-boov)* .... ladies' footware
женская одежда *(zhen-skah-yah)(ah-dyezh-dah)* ... ladies' clothing
женские головные уборы *(zhen-skee-yeh)(gah-lahv-nih-yeh)(oo-bohr-ih)* .... ladies' hats
жёлтый *(zhyol-tee)* .... yellow
жить *(zheet)* .... to live, to reside
журнал *(zhoor-nahl)* .... journal, magazine
журналы *(zhoor-nah-lih)* .... journals, magazines
журналист *(zhoor-nah-leest)* .... journalist

З

за *(zah)* .... behind
завтра *(zahv-trah)* .... tomorrow
завтрак *(zahv-trahk)* .... breakfast
заказ *(zah-kahz)* .... reservations
заказывать *(zah-kah-zih-vaht)* .... to order, to reserve
закрывается *(zah-krih-vah-yet-syah)* .... closes
закрыта *(zah-krih-tah)* .... closed
закуски *(zah-koo-skee)* .... appetizers, snacks
занавес *(zah-nahv-yes)* .... curtain
занимает *(zah-nee-mah-yet)* .... it occupies, it takes up
занято *(zahn-yah-tah)* .... busy, occupied
запад *(zah-pahd)* .... west
запасной выход *(zah-pahs-noy)(vwee-hahd)* ..... emergency exit
запечённое *(zahp-yeh-chyohn-nah-yeh)* .... baked
заплатить за *(zah-plah-teet)(zah)* .... to pay for
звонить *(zvah-neet)* .... to phone
здесь *(zdyes)* .... here
здоров *(zdah-rohv)* .... healthy
зелёный *(zyel-yoh-nee)* .... green
зеркало *(zyair-kah-lah)* .... mirror
зеркала *(zyair-kah-lah)* .... mirrors
зимой *(zee-moy)* .... in winter
знать *(znaht)* .... to know
вы знаете *(vwee)(znah-yet-yeh)* .... you know
зовут *(zah-voot)* .... is called
как зовут *(kahk)(zah-voot)* .... what is (someone's) name
меня зовут *(men-yah)(zah-voot)* .... I am called, my name is
зона *(zoh-nah)* .... zone
зонтик *(zohn-teek)* .... umbrella
зонты *(zahn-tih)* .... umbrellas
зоопарк *(zah-ah-park)* .... zoo
зубная паста *(zoob-nah-yah)(pahs-tah)* .... toothpaste
зубная щётка *(zoob-nah-yah)(shchoht-kah)* .... toothbrush

И

и *(ee)* .... and
игрушки *(ee-groosh-kee)* .... toys
идти *(eed-tee)* .... to go, to walk (to a destination)
он/она идёт *(ee-dyoht)* .... he / she goes, walks
идёт дождь *(ee-dyoht)(dohzhd)* .... it rains
идёт снег *(ee-dyoht)(snyeg)* .... it snows
из *(eez)* .... out of, from
извините *(eez-vee-neet-yeh)* .... excuse me
изучать *(ee-zoo-chaht)* .... to learn
изучайте! *(ee-zoo-chay-tee)* .... learn!
икра *(ee-krah)* .... caviar
или *(ee-lee)* .... or
имена *(ee-myen-ah)* .... names
импортный *(eem-part-nee)* .... imported
Индия *(een-dee-yah)* .... India
индустриальный *(een-doo-stree-ahl-nee)* .... industrial
инженер *(een-zhyen-yair)* .... engineer
иностранный *(ee-nah-strahn-nee)* .... foreign
инспектор *(een-spyek-tar)* .... inspector
институт *(een-stee-toot)* .... institute
инструктор *(een-strook-tar)* .... instructor
инструкции *(een-strook-tsee-ee)* .... instructions
инструмент *(een-stroo-myent)* .... instrument
интеллигент *(een-tyel-lee-gyent)* .... intellectual
интервью *(een-tyair-view)* .... interview
интерес *(een-tyair-yes)* .... interest
интернациональный *(een-tyair-naht-see-ah-nahl-nee)* ... international
информация *(een-far-maht-see-yah)* .... information
искать *(ees-kaht)* .... to look for
Исландия *(ees-lahn-dee-yah)* .... Iceland
Испания *(ee-spahn-ee-yah)* .... Spain
Испанию *(ee-spahn-ee-yoo)* .... Spain
история *(ees-toh-ree-yah)* .... history
Италия *(ee-tah-lee-yah)* .... Italy
Италию *(ee-tah-lee-yoo)* .... Italy
их зовут *(eehk)(zah-voot)* .... their name is
июль *(ee-yool)* .... July
июле *(ee-yool-yeh)* .... July
июнь *(ee-yoon)* .... June

К

к себе *(kuh)(syeb-yeh)* .... pull (doors)
кабина *(kah-bee-nah)* .... cabin, booth
кабинет *(kah-bee-nyet)* .... study
Казахстан *(kah-zahk-stahn)* .... Kazakstan
казах *(kah-zahk)* .... Kazak
как *(kahk)* .... how
Как дела? *(kahk)(dee-lah)* .... how are things? how are you?
Как вас зовут? *(kahk)(vahs)(zah-voot)* .... what is your name?
какая *(kah-kah-yah)* .... what kind of, how is
какао *(kah-kah-oh)* .... cocoa
какой *(kah-koy)* .... what
календарь *(kah-lyen-dar)* .... calendar
камера *(kah-myair-ah)* .... cell, chamber
камера хранения *(kah-myair-ah)(hrah-nyen-ee-yah)* .... left-luggage office
Канада *(kah-nah-dah)* .... Canada
Канаду *(kah-nah-doo)* .... Canada
канадец *(kah-nah-dyets)* .... Canadian
канал *(kah-nahl)* .... canal
канарейка *(kah-nah-ray-kah)* .... canary
кандидат *(kahn-dee-daht)* .... candidate
канцтовары *(kahnt-stah-vah-rih)* .... stationery store
капитал *(kah-pee-tahl)* .... capital (money)
капиталист *(kah-pee-tah-leest)* .... capitalist

карамель *(kah-rah-myel)* . . . . caramel
карандаш *(kah-rahn-dahsh)* . . . . pencil
карие *(kah-ree-yeh)* . . . . light brown
карта *(kar-tah)* . . . . map
карту *(kar-too)* . . . . map
карты *(kar-tih)* . . . . maps
картина *(kar-tee-nah)* . . . . picture
касса *(kahs-sah)* . . . . ticket machine, cashier, tickets
кассу *(kahs-soo)* . . . . booking office, cashier
кассиру *(kahs-see-roo)* . . . . cashier
католик *(kah-toh-leek)* . . . . Catholic man
католичка *(kah-tah-leech-kah)* . . . . Catholic woman
кафе *(kah-fyeh)* . . . . cafe
квитанция *(kvee-tahn-tsee-yah)* . . . . receipt
керамика *(kee-rahm-ee-kah)* . . . . ceramics
Киев *(kee-yev)* . . . . Kiev
кило *(kee-loh)* . . . . kilo
кино *(kee-noh)* . . . . cinema
киоск *(kee-ohsk)* . . . . newsstand
класс *(klahs)* . . . . class
классик *(klahs-seek)* . . . . classic
клоун *(kloh-oon)* . . . . clown
книга *(kuh-nee-gah)* . . . . book
книги *(kuh-nee-gee)* . . . . book, bookstore
книгу *(kuh-nee-goo)* . . . . book
ковёр *(kahv-yor)* . . . . carpet
ковры *(kahv-rih)* . . . . carpets
когда *(kahg-dah)* . . . . when
кожаные товары *(koh-zhah-nih-yeh)(tah-var-ih)* . . . leather goods
колбаса *(kahl-bah-sah)* . . . . sausage
колготки *(kahl-goht-kee)* . . . . pantyhose
коллекция *(kahl-yekt-see-yah)* . . . . collection
командир *(kah-mahn-deer)* . . . . commander
комбинация *(kahm-bee-naht-see-yah)* . . . . slip
комедия *(kah-myeh-dee-yah)* . . . . comedy
комиссар *(kah-mees-sar)* . . . . commissar
коммунист *(kahm-moo-neest)* . . . . communist
комната *(kohm-nah-tah)* . . . . room
комнате *(kohm-nah-tyeh)* . . . . room
комнаты *(kohm-nah-tih)* . . . . room
компас *(kohm-pahs)* . . . . compass
композитор *(kahm-pah-zee-tar)* . . . . composer
компьютер *(kahmp-yoo-tyer)* . . . . computer
кому *(koh-moo)* . . . . to whom (on envelopes)
конверт *(kahn-vyairt)* . . . . envelope
конверты *(kahn-vyair-tih)* . . . . envelopes
конверты-авиа *(kahn-vyair-tih-ah-vee-ah)* . . . airmail envelopes
коньяк *(kahn-yahk)* . . . . cognac
конференция *(kahn-fyair-yent-see-yah)* . . . . . conference
концерт *(kahn-tsairt)* . . . . concert
корзина *(kar-zee-nah)* . . . . basket
коричневый *(kah-reech-nyeh-vwee)* . . . . brown
короткая *(kah-roht-kah-yah)* . . . . short
корт *(kort)* . . . . court (tennis)
косметика *(kahs-myeh-tee-kah)* . . . . cosmetics
костюм *(kahst-yoom)* . . . . suit
кот *(koht)* . . . . cat
который час? *(kah-toh-ree)(chahs)* . . . . . . what time is it?
кофе *(koh-fyeh)* . . . . coffee
кошка *(kohsh-kah)* . . . . cat
кошку *(kohsh-koo)* . . . . cat
краб *(krahb)* . . . . crab
красивых *(krah-see-vik)* . . . . pretty
красный *(krahs-nee)* . . . . red
кредитная карточка *(kreh-deet-nah-yah)(kar-tahch-kah)* . . . .
. . . . credit card
Кремль *(kreml)* . . . . Kremlin
кровать *(krah-vaht)* . . . . bed
кровати *(krah-vah-tee)* . . . . bed
кроссовки *(krahs-sohv-kee)* . . . . tennis shoes
кто *(ktoh)* . . . . who
Куба *(koo-bah)* . . . . Cuba
куда *(koo-dah)* . . . . where (on envelopes)
культуры *(kool-toor-ih)* . . . . cultural
купальный костюм *(koo-pahl-nee)(kahst-yoom)* . . . . . . swimsuit
купальные костюмы *(koo-pahl-nih-yeh)(kahst-yoom-ih)* . swimsuits
купить *(koo-peet)* . . . . to buy
кухня *(koohk-nyah)* . . . . kitchen
кухне *(koohk-nyeh)* . . . . kitchen

Кыргызстан *(kir-geez-stahn)* . . . . Kyrgyzstan
кыргыз *(kir-geez)* . . . . Kyrgyz

Л

лаборатория *(lah-bah-rah-toh-ree-yah)* . . . . laboratory
лампа *(lahm-pah)* . . . . lamp, light
лампы *(lahm-pih)* . . . . lamps
Латвия *(laht-vee-yah)* . . . . Latvia
латыш *(lah-tish)* . . . . Latvian
Ленинград *(lyen-een-grahd)* . . . . . . Leningrad (now St. Petersburg)
лететь *(lee-tyet)* . . . . to fly
летом *(lyet-ahm)* . . . . in summer
лимон *(lee-mohn)* . . . . lemon
лимонад *(lee-mah-nahd)* . . . . lemonade
линия *(lee-nee-yah)* . . . . line
линии *(lee-nee-ee)* . . . . lines (transportation)
линию *(lee-nee-yoo)* . . . . lines
литература *(lee-tyair-ah-too-rah)* . . . . literature
Литва *(leet-vah)* . . . . Lithuania
литовец *(lee-toh-vyets)* . . . . Lithuanian
литр *(lee-ter)* . . . . liter
лифчик *(leef-cheek)* . . . . brassiere
ложка *(lohzh-kah)* . . . . spoon
любят *(loob-yaht)* . . . . (they) love
люди *(loo-dee)* . . . . people

М

магазин *(mah-gah-zeen)* . . . . store
магазины *(mah-gah-zeen-ih)* . . . . stores
май *(my)* . . . . May
майка *(my-kah)* . . . . t-shirt, undershirt
максимальная скорость *(mahk-see-mahl-nah-yah)(skoh-rahst)* . . .
. . . . speed limit
маленькая *(mah-lyen-kah-yah)* . . . . small
маленькие *(mah-lyen-kee-ee)* . . . . small
маленький *(mah-lyen-kee)* . . . . small
мало *(mah-lah)* . . . . little
Мариинский театр *(mah-reen-skee)(tee-ah-ter)* . . Mariinsky Theater
марка *(mar-kah)* . . . . stamp
марки *(mar-kee)* . . . . stamps
марок *(mar-ahk)* . . . . stamps
март *(mart)* . . . . March
масло *(mah-slah)* . . . . butter
масса *(mahs-sah)* . . . . mass
мастер *(mahs-tyair)* . . . . master
математика *(mah-tyeh-mah-tee-kah)* . . . . mathematics
материя *(mah-tyair-ee-yah)* . . . . material
матрёшки *(mah-tryohsh-kah)* . . . . Russian dolls
матч *(mahtch)* . . . . match (game)
мать *(maht)* . . . . mother
машина *(mah-shee-nah)* . . . . machine (car)
машина напрокат *(mah-shee-nah)(nah-prah-kaht)* . . . . rental car
мебель *(myeh-byel)* . . . . furniture
медаль *(myeh-dahl)* . . . . medal
медик *(myeh-deek)* . . . . medic
медицина *(myeh-deet-see-nah)* . . . . medicine
медленно *(myed-lyen-nah)* . . . . slow, slowly
между *(myezh-doo)* . . . . between
междугородний *(myezh-doo-gah-rohd-nee)* . . . .
. . . . long-distance, inter-city
международный *(myezh-doo-nah-rohd-nee)* . . . . international (calls)
Международный женский день *(myezh-doo-nah-rohd-nee)(zhen-skee)(dyen)* . . . . International Women's Day
мелодия *(myeh-loh-dee-yah)* . . . . melody
меню *(men-yoo)* . . . . menu
меня зовут *(men-yah)(zah-voot)* . . . . . I am called, my name is
местный *(myes-nee)* . . . . domestic, internal
место *(myes-tah)* . . . . seat, place
месяц *(myeh-syets)* . . . . month
месяцев *(myeh-syet-syev)* . . . . months
месяцы *(myeh-syet-sih)* . . . . months
металл *(myeh-tahl)* . . . . metal
метод *(myeh-tahd)* . . . . method
метро *(myeh-troh)* . . . . metro, subway
механик *(myeh-hah-neek)* . . . . mechanic
микрофон *(mee-krah-fohn)* . . . . microphone
милиция *(mee-leet-see-yah)* . . . . police
миллион *(meel-lee-ohn)* . . . . million
миниатюра *(mee-nee-ah-tyoo-rah)* . . . . miniature
минут *(mee-noot)* . . . . minutes

минуте *(mee-noot-yeh)* . . . . minutes
мира *(mee-rah)* . . . . peace
миссия *(mees-see-yah)* . . . . mission
митинг *(mee-teeng)* . . . . meeting
мне *(men-yeh)* . . . . to me
мне нужно *(men-yeh)(noozh-nah)* . . . . I need
много *(mnoh-gah)* . . . . a lot, many
модель *(mah-dyel)* . . . . model
мой *(moy)* . . . . my
Молдова *(mahl-doh-vah)* . . . . Moldova
молдованин *(mahl-dah-vah-neen)* . . . . Moldavian
молодая баранина *(mah-lah-dah-yah)(bah-rah-nee-nah)* . . . . lamb
молодой *(mah-lah-doy)* . . . . young
молоко *(mah-lah-koh)* . . . . milk, dairy
молока *(mah-lah-kah)* . . . . milk
момент *(mah-myent)* . . . . moment
мороженое *(mah-roh-zhen-ah-yeh)* . . . . ice cream
Москва *(mahsk-vah)* . . . . Moscow
Москву *(mahsk-voo)* . . . . Moscow
Москвы *(mahsk-vih)* . . . . Moscow
мотор *(mah-tor)* . . . . motor
мотоцикл *(mah-tah-tsee-kul)* . . . . motorcycle
мочь *(mohch)* . . . . to be able to, can
я могу *(yah)(mah-goo)* . . . . I can
можете *(mohzh-yet-yeh)* . . . . (you) can, are able to
мужчина *(moozh-chee-nah)* . . . . man
мужская одежда *(moozh-skah-yah)(ah-dyezh-dah)* . . men's clothing
мужская обувь *(moozh-skah-yah)(oh-boov)* . . . . . . men's footware
мужские головные уборы *(moozh-skee-yeh)(gah-lahv-nih-yeh)*
. . . . *(oo-bohr-ih)* . . . . men's hats
мужской *(moozh-skoy)* . . . . men's (restroom)
муза *(moo-zah)* . . . . muse
музей *(moo-zay)* . . . . museum
музея *(moo-zyeh-yah)* . . . . museum
музыка *(moo-zih-kah)* . . . . music
музыкальные товары *(moo-zih-kahl-nih-yeh)(tah-var-ih)* . . . .
. . . . musical articles
мусульманин *(moo-sool-mah-neen)* . . . . Moslem man
мусульманка *(moo-sool-mahn-kah)* . . . . Moslem woman
мы *(mwee)* . . . . we
мы хотим купить *(mwee)(hah-teem)(koo-peet)* . . we would like to buy
мыло *(mwee-lah)* . . . . soap
мясо *(myah-sah)* . . . . meat
мясо-грилль *(myah-sah-greel)* . . . . grilled
мясной магазин *(myahs-noy)(mah-gah-zeen)* . . . . . . butcher shop

Н

на *(nah)* . . . . on, into
на углу *(nah)(oo-gloo)* . . . . on corner
набережная (наб.) *(nah-byair-yesh-nah-yah)* . . . . . embankment
наверху *(nah-vyair-hoo)* . . . . upstairs
над *(nahd)* . . . . over
название *(nahz-vah-nee-yeh)* . . . . name
названия *(nahz-vah-nee-yah)* . . . . names
налево *(nah-lyev-ah)* . . . . to the left
нам нужно *(nahm)(noozh-nah)* . . . . we need
напитки *(nah-peet-kee)* . . . . beverages
напишите *(nah-pee-sheet-yeh)* . . . . write out
направо *(nah-prah-vah)* . . . . to the right
нас зовут *(nahs)(zah-voot)* . . . . our name is
находите *(nah-hoh-deet-yet)* . . . . (you) find
нация *(naht-see-yah)* . . . . nation
начинается *(nah-chee-nah-yet-syah)* . . . . begins
не *(nyeh)* . . . . not, no
не надо *(nyeh)(nah-dah)* . . . . (it is) not right
неделя *(nee-dyel-yah)* . . . . week
недели *(nee-dyel-ee)* . . . . week
нейлон *(nay-lohn)* . . . . nylon
немецкий *(nee-myet-skee)* . . . . German
несерьёзный *(nyeh-syair-yohz-nee)* . . . . not serious
нет *(nyet)* . . . . no, not
Нижний Новгород *(neezh-nee)(nohv-gah-rahd)* . . . Nizhny Novgorod
никель *(neek-yehl)* . . . . nickel
но *(noh)* . . . . but
Новгород *(nohv-gah-rahd)* . . . . Novgorod
новых *(noh-vik)* . . . . new
новые *(noh-vih-yeh)* . . . . new
новым *(noh-vim)* . . . . new
нож *(nohzh)* . . . . knife
ноль *(nohl)* . . . . zero

номер *(nohm-yair)* . . . . number (room), hotel room
Норвегия *(nar-vyeh-gee-yah)* . . . . Norway
норма *(nor-mah)* . . . . norm, standard
нормальная *(nar-mahl-nah-yah)* . . . . normal
нос *(nohs)* . . . . nose
носильщик *(nah-seel-shcheek)* . . . . porter
носки *(nah-skee)* . . . . socks
ночь *(nohch)* . . . . night
ночная рубашка *(nahch-nah-yah)(roo-bahsh-kah)* . . . . . nightshirt
ноябрь *(nah-yah-bair)* . . . . November
нужно *(noozh-nah)* . . . . need
мне нужно *(men-yeh)(noozh-nah)* . . . . I need

О

обгон запрещён *(ahb-gohn)(zah-presh-chyohn)* . . . . no passing
обед *(ah-byed)* . . . . meal, mid-day meal, dinner
объезд *(ahb-yezd)* . . . . detour
овощи *(oh-vahsh-chee)* . . . . vegetables, greengrocer
одежда *(ah-dyezh-dah)* . . . . clothes
одежды *(ah-dyezh-dih)* . . . . clothes
Одесса *(ah-des-sah)* . . . . Odessa
одеяло *(ah-dee-yah-lah)* . . . . blanket
одеялом *(ah-dee-yah-lahm)* . . . . blanket
один *(ah-deen)* . . . . one
одиннадцать *(ah-deen-nud-tset)* . . . . eleven
одну минуту *(ahd-noo)(mee-noo-too)* . . . . just a minute
окно *(ahk-noh)* . . . . window
октябрь *(ahk-tyah-bair)* . . . . October
оленина *(ahl-yeh-nee-nah)* . . . . venison
олимпиада *(ah-leem-pee-ah-dah)* . . . . Olympics
он *(ohn)* . . . . he
она *(ah-nah)* . . . . she
они *(ah-nee)* . . . . they
опера *(oh-pyair-ah)* . . . . opera
оплатить *(ah-plah-teet)* . . . . to pay
оранжевый *(ah-rahn-zheh-vwee)* . . . . orange (color)
органист *(ar-gah-neest)* . . . . organist
оркестр *(ar-kyes-tair)* . . . . orchestra
осенью *(oh-syen-yoo)* . . . . in autumn
остановка *(ahs-tah-nohv-kah)* . . . . stop
остановка автобуса *(ahs-tah-nohv-kah)(ahv-toh-boo-sah)* . . . .
. . . . bus stop
остановка трамвая *(ahs-tah-nohv-kah)(trahm-vah-yah)*
. . . . trolley stop
от себя *(aht)(syeb-yah)* . . . . push (doors)
отварное *(aht-var-noh-yeh)* . . . . boiled
ответы *(aht-vyet-ih)* . . . . answers
отель *(ah-tyel)* . . . . hotel
отец *(aht-yets)* . . . . father
отца *(aht-tsah)* . . . . father
открывается *(aht-krih-vah-yet-syah)* . . . . opens
открыта *(aht-krih-tah)* . . . . open
открытка *(aht-krit-kah)* . . . . postcard
открытки *(aht-krit-kee)* . . . . postcards
открытку *(aht-krit-koo)* . . . . postcard
открыток *(aht-krih-tahk)* . . . . postcards
отправление *(aht-prahv-lyen-ee-yeh)* . . . . . . departures
отправления *(aht-prahv-lyen-ee-yah)* . . . . . . departures
отходить *(aht-hah-deet)* . . . . . to depart (vehicles)
офицер *(ah-feet-syair)* . . . . officer
официальный *(ah-feet-see-ahl-nee)* . . . . official
официант *(ah-feet-see-ahnt)* . . . . waiter
официантка *(ah-feet-see-ahnt-kah)* . . . . waitress
очень *(oh-chen)* . . . . very
очки *(ahch-kee)* . . . . eyeglasses

П

павильон *(pah-veel-yohn)* . . . . pavilion
пакет *(pah-kyet)* . . . . package
Пакистан *(pah-kee-stahn)* . . . . Pakistan
пальто *(pahl-toh)* . . . . overcoat
парад *(pah-rahd)* . . . . parade
парикмахерская *(pah-reek-mahl-yairs-kah-yah)* . . . . . hairdresser
парк *(park)* . . . . park
парламент *(par-lah-myent)* . . . . parliament
партия *(par-tee-yah)* . . . . party
паспорт *(pahs-part)* . . . . passport
пассажир *(pahs-sah-zheer)* . . . . passenger
Пасха *(pahs-hkah)* . . . . Easter
перед *(pyeh-red)* . . . . in front of

перец (pyeh-rets) . . . . pepper
перчатки (pyair-chaht-kee) . . . . gloves
Петербург (pyeh-tyair-boorg) . . . . St. Petersburg
пиво (pee-vah) . . . . beer
пиджак (peed-zhahk) . . . . jacket, blazer
пижама (pee-zhah-mah) . . . . pajamas
пирог (pee-rohg) . . . . cake, pie, pastry
пирожки (pee-rahzh-kee) . . . . . . pastries, small cakes
пирожные (pee-rohzh-nee-yeh) . . . pastries, small cakes
писать (pee-saht) . . . . to write
письмо (pees-moh) . . . . letter
пить (peet) . . . . to drink
платить (plah-teet) . . . . to pay
платить за (plah-teet)(zah) . . . . to pay for
платок (plah-tohk) . . . . handkerchief, shawl
платформа (plaht-for-mah) . . . . platform
платье (plaht-yeh) . . . . skirt
плащ (plahshch) . . . . raincoat
плита (plee-tah) . . . . stove
птица (pteet-sah) . . . . poultry
плохо (ploh-hah) . . . . bad
плохая погода (plah-hah-yah)(pah-go-dah) . bad weather
площадь (пл.) (plahsh-chahd) . . . . square
по (poh) . . . . on
повторять (pahv-tar-yaht) . . . . to repeat
повторите (pahv-tah-reet-yeh) . . . . repeat!
поговорить (pah-gah-vah-reet) . . . . to speak
погода (pah-go-dah) . . . . weather
погоды (pah-go-dih) . . . . weather
под (pohd) . . . . under
подвал (pahd-vahl) . . . . basement
подушка (pah-doosh-kah) . . . . pillow
поезд (poh-yezd) . . . . train
поезда (poh-yez-dah) . . . . trains
поездка (pah-yezd-kah) . . . . trip, journey
поехать (pah-yek-haht) . . . . to go
пожалуйста (pah-zhahl-oos-tah) . . . please, you're welcome
пожар (pah-zhar) . . . . fire
позвонить (pah-zvah-neet) . . . . to phone, to call
поздравления (pahz-drahv-lyen-ee-yah) . congratulations
позже (pohzh-yeh) . . . . later
позиция (pah-zeet-see-yah) . . . . position
показывать (pah-kah-zih-vaht) . . . . to show
покупать (pah-koo-paht) . . . . to buy
полиция (pah-leet-see-yah) . . . . police
половина (pah-lah-vee-nah) . . . . half
полотенца (pah-lah-tyent-sah) . . . . towels
Польша (pohl-shah) . . . . Poland
понедельник (pah-nee-dyel-neek) . . . . Monday
понимать (pah-nee-maht) . . . . to understand
по-английски (pah-ahn-glee-skee) . . . . . . in English
по-русски (pah-roos-skee) . . . . in Russian
порт (port) . . . . port
портрет (part-ryet) . . . . portrait
послать (pah-slaht) . . . . to send
постельное бельё (pah-styel-nah-yeh)(byel-yoh) . . . bedding
посылать (pah-sih-laht) . . . . to send
посылка (pah-sil-kah) . . . . package
посылки (pah-sil-kee) . . . . packages
посылку (pah-sil-koo) . . . . package
потом (pah-tohm) . . . . then
почему (pah-chee-moo) . . . . why
почта (poach-tah) . . . . mail, post office
почту (poach-too) . . . . mail, post office
почты (poach-tih) . . . . post office
почтовый ящик (pahch-toh-vee)(yahsh-chik) . . mailbox
пояса (pah-yah-sah) . . . . belts
православная (prah-vah-slahv-nah-yah) . . . Orthodox woman
православный (prah-vah-slahv-nee) . . . Orthodox man
прачечная (prahch-yech-nah-yah) . . . . laundry
прибытие (pree-bit-ee-yeh) . . . . arrival
прибытия (pree-bit-ee-yah) . . . . arrivals
пригородов (pree-gah-rah-dahv) . . . . suburbs
пригородные (pree-gah-rahd-nee-yeh) . . . . suburban
приезжать (pree-yez-zhaht) . . . . to arrive
примеры (pree-myair-ih) . . . . examples
принадлежности туалета (pree-nahd-lehzh-nah-stee)(too-ahl-yet-ah) . . . . toiletries
приходить (pree-hah-deet) . . . . to arrive (vehicles)
придёт (pree-dyoht) . . . . arrives (a vehicle)

прилетите (pree-lee-teet-yeh) . . . . . . (you) arrive by plane
приятного аппетита! (pree-yaht-nah-vah)(ah-peh-tee-tah) . . . . enjoy your meal, good appetite
правильное (prah-veel-nah-yeh) . . . . correct
программа (prah-grahm-mah) . . . . program
прогресс (prahg-ryes) . . . . progress
продавать (prah-dah-vaht) . . . . to sell
продмаг (prahd-mahg) . . . . food store
продукт (prah-dookt) . . . . product
проект (prah-yekt) . . . . project
пройдёте (prah-ee-dyoht-yeh) . . . . go!
проспект (пр.) (prah-spekt) . . . . . avenue, boulevard
профессия (prah-fyes-see-yah) . . . . profession
профессор (prah-fyes-sar) . . . . professor
процент (praht-syent) . . . . percent
прочитать (prah-chee-taht) . . . . to read
прямо (pryah-mah) . . . . straight ahead
птица (pteet-sah) . . . . poultry
путешественник (poot-yeh-shest-vyen-neek) . . . traveler
путешествовать (poot-yeh-shest-vah-vaht) . . . to travel
путь (poot) . . . . line, route
пятница (pyaht-neet-sah) . . . . Friday
пять (pyaht) . . . . five
пятнадцать (pyaht-nahd-tset) . . . . fifteen
пятьдесят (peed-dyes-yaht) . . . . fifty

Р

радио (rah-dee-oh) . . . . radio
разговор по телефону (rahz-gah-vor)(pah)(teh-leh-foh-noo) . . . . telephone conversation
размер (rahz-myair) . . . . size
ракета (rah-kyet-ah) . . . . rocket
ранг (rahng) . . . . rank
рапорт (rah-port) . . . . report
расписание (rah-spee-sah-nee-yeh) . . schedule, timetable
расчёска (rahs-chohs-kah) . . . . comb
револьвер (ryeh-vahl-vyair) . . . . revolver
революция (ryeh-vahl-yoot-see-yah) . . . . revolution
регистрация (ryeh-geest-raht-see-yah) . . . registration
рекорд (ryeh-kord) . . . . record
религия (ree-lee-gee-yah) . . . . religion
религии (ree-lee-gee-ee) . . . . religions
ресторан (res-tah-rahn) . . . . restaurant
ресторане (res-tah-rahn-yeh) . . . . restaurant
Рига (ree-gah) . . . . Riga
родители (rah-dee-tee-lee) . . . . parents
родственники (rohd-stveen-nee-kee) . . . . relatives
розовый (roh-zah-vwee) . . . . pink
Россия (rahs-see-yah) . . . . Russia
Россию (rahs-see-yoo) . . . . Russia
России (rahs-see-ee) . . . . Russia
российского (rahs-see-skah-vah) . . . . Russian
рубашка (roo-bahsh-kah) . . . . shirt
рубль (roo-bil) . . . . ruble
рублей (roo-blay) . . . . rubles
русский (roos-skee) . . . . Russian
по-русски (pah-roos-skee) . . . . in Russian
русские (roos-skee-yeh) . . . . Russian
русское (roos-skah-yeh) . . . . Russian
ручка (rooch-kah) . . . . pen
рыба (rih-bah) . . . . fish
рыбу (rih-boo) . . . . fish
рыбный рынок (rib-nee)(rin-ahk) . . . . . fish market
рынок (rin-ahk) . . . . market
рынке (rin-kyeh) . . . . market
рядом с (ryah-dahm)(suh) . . . . next to

С

с (suh) . . . . with
сад (sahd) . . . . garden
салат (sah-laht) . . . . salad
салфетка (sahl-fyet-kah) . . . . napkin
самовар (sah-mah-var) . . . . samovar
самолёт (sah-mahl-yoht) . . . . airplane
самолёте (sah-mahl-yoht-yeh) . . . . airplane
сандалии (sahn-dahl-ee-ee) . . . . sandals
Санкт-Петербург (sahnkt-pyeh-tyair-boorg) . St. Petersburg
сапоги (sah-pah-gee) . . . . boots
свинина (svee-nee-nah) . . . . pork
свитер (svee-tyair) . . . . sweater

113

свободно *(svah-bohd-nah)* .... free, available
сделать *(suh-dyeh-laht)* .... to do
сдача *(sdah-chah)* .... change
сдачу *(sdah-choo)* .... change
север *(syev-yair)* .... north
Северная Америка *(syev-yair-nah-yah)(ah-myeh-ree-kah)* .... North America
Северная Дакота *(syev-yair-nah-yah)(dah-koh-tah)* .. North Dakota
Северная Каролина *(syev-yair-nah-yah)(kah-rah-lee-nah)* .... North Carolina
Северная Корея *(syev-yair-nah-yah)(kah-reh-yah)* .. North Korea
сегодня *(see-vohd-nyah)* .... today
сезон *(syeh-zone)* .... season
секретарь *(syek-ryair-tar)* .... secretary
секунда *(see-koon-dah)* .... second
семинар *(syem-ee-nar)* .... seminar
семь *(syem)* .... seven
семнадцать *(sim-nahd-tset)* .... seventeen
семьдесят *(syem-dyes-yet)* .... seventy
семья *(syem-yah)* .... family
сентябрь *(syen-tyah-bair)* .... September
серый *(syeh-ree)* .... gray
сестра *(see-strah)* .... sister
сигара *(see-gah-rah)* .... cigar
сигарета *(see-gah-ryet-ah)* .... cigarette
сидит *(see-deet)* .... it fits
симфония *(seem-foh-nee-yah)* .... symphony
синий *(see-nee)* .... blue
сколько *(skohl-kah)* .... how much
сколько времени? *(skohl-kah)(vreh-mee-nee)* ..... what time is it?
сколько это стоит? *(skohl-kah)(et-tah)(stoy-eet)* .... how much does this cost?
скорая помощь *(skoh-rah-yah)(poh-mashch)* .... emergency medical help
сладкие блюда *(slahd-kee-yeh)(bloo-dah)* .... sweets
слово *(sloh-vah)* .... word
слов *(slohv)* .... words
слова *(slah-vah)* .... words
словарь *(slah-var)* .... dictionary
словаре *(slah-var-yeh)* .... dictionary
служба газа *(sloozh-bah)(gah-zah)* .... heating gas service
Смоленск *(smahl-yensk)* .... Smolensk
снег *(snyeg)* .... snow
собака *(sah-bah-kah)* .... dog
собаку *(sah-bah-koo)* .... dog
Собор Василия Блаженного *(sah-bohr)(vah-see-lee-yah)(blah-zhen-nah-vah)* .... St. Basil's Cathedral
советский *(sah-vyet-skee)* .... Soviet
Советский Союз *(sah-vyet-skee)(say-yooz)* .... Soviet Union
сок *(sohk)* .... juice
соль *(sole)* .... salt
сорок *(so-rahk)* .... forty
сосиски *(sah-see-skee)* .... sausages
сот *(soht)* .... one hundred
соус *(soh-oos)* .... sauce
спальня *(spahl-nyah)* .... bedroom
спальне *(spahl-nyeh)* .... bedroom
спальню *(spahl-nyoo)* .... bedroom
спальный вагон *(spahl-nee)(vah-gohn)* .... sleeping wagon
спасибо *(spah-see-bah)* .... thank you
спать *(spaht)* .... to sleep
спиртные напитки *(speert-nih-yeh)(nah-peet-kee)* .... alcoholic beverages
спокойной ночи *(spah-koy-nay)(noh-chee)* .... good night
спортивные товары *(spar-teev-nih-yeh)(tah-var-ih)* .. sporting goods
справочное бюро *(sprah-vahch-nah-yeh)(byoo-roh)* .... information bureau
среда *(sree-dah)* .... Wednesday
стадион *(stah-dee-ohn)* .... stadium
стакан *(stah-kahn)* .... glass
станция *(stahnt-see-yah)* .... station
станция метро *(stahnt-see-ah)(myeh-troh)* .... metro station
старый *(stah-ree)* .... old
старейший *(star-yeh-shee)* .... oldest
старт *(start)* .... start
стирать *(stee-raht)* .... to wash, to clean (clothes)
стоит *(stoy-eet)* .... costs
сто *(stoh)* .... one hundred
стол *(stohl)* .... table
столовая *(stah-loh-vah-yah)* .... cafeteria, dining room
стоп *(stohp)* .... stop
стоянка *(stah-yahn-kah)* .... parking lot, taxi stand
стоянка запрещена *(stoh-yahn-kah)(zah-presh-chen-ah)* .. no parking
страница *(strah-neet-sah)* .... page
страниц *(strah-neets)* .... pages
странице *(strah-neet-seh)* .... page
студент *(stoo-dyent)* .... student
стул *(stool)* .... chair
суббота *(soo-boh-tah)* .... Saturday
сувениры *(soo-veh-neer-ih)* .... souvenirs
сумка *(soom-kah)* .... purse, handbag
сумму *(soom-moo)* .... sum
суп *(soop)* .... soup
Счастливого пути! *(schahst-lee-vah-vah)(poo-tee)* .. Have a good trip!
счёт *(shyoht)* .... bill
счета *(shyeh-tah)* .... bills
счёте *(shyoht-yeh)* .... bill
США *(seh-sheh-ah)* .... the United States
сын *(sin)* .... son
сына *(sin-ah)* .... son
сыр *(seer)* .... cheese

Т

табак *(tah-bahk)* .... tobacco
Таджикистан *(tahd-zheek-ee-stahn)* .... Tajikistan
таджик *(tahd-zheek)* .... Tajik
такси *(tahk-see)* .... taxi
там *(tahm)* .... there
таможня *(tah-mohzh-nyah)* .... customs
тапочки *(tah-poach-kee)* .... slippers
тарелка *(tar-yel-kah)* .... plate
Ташкент *(tahsh-kyent)* .... Tashkent
театр *(tee-ah-ter)* .... theater
Театр Кирова *(tee-ah-ter)(kee-rah-vah)* .... Kirov Theater
телевизор *(teh-leh-vee-zar)* .... TV set
телеграмма *(teh-leh-grahm-mah)* .... telegram
телескоп *(teh-leh-skope)* .... telescope
телефон *(teh-leh-fohn)* .... telephone
телефон-автомат *(teh-leh-fohn-ahv-tah-maht)* ... public telephone
телефонист *(teh-leh-fahn-eest)* .... operator
телефонная книга *(teh-leh-fohn-nah-yah)(kuh-nee-gah)* .... telephone book
телятина *(tyel-yah-tee-nah)* .... veal
температура *(tem-pee-rah-too-rah)* .... temperature
температура замерзания *(tem-pee-rah-too-rah)(zah-myair-zah-nee-yah)* .... freezing point
теннис *(tyen-nees)* .... tennis
теперь *(tyep-yair)* .... now
терять *(tyair-yaht)* .... to lose
тёмные очки *(tyohm-nih-yeh)(ahch-kee)* .... sunglasses
тётя *(tyoh-tyah)* .... aunt
тогда *(tahg-dah)* .... then
тоже *(toh-zheh)* .... also
товары для кухни *(tah-vah-rih)(dil-yah)(koohk-nee)* .. kitchen wares
томат *(tah-maht)* .... tomato
тост *(tohst)* .... toast
трамвай *(trahm-vy)* .... streetcar, trolley
три *(tree)* .... three
тридцать *(treed-tset)* .... thirty
тринадцать *(tree-nahd-tset)* .... thirteen
триста *(tree-stah)* .... three hundred
трусы *(troo-sih)* .... underpants
туалет *(too-ahl-yet)* .... toilet
туалетные *(too-ahl-yet-nih-yeh)* .... toiletries
туда и обратно *(too-dah)(ee)(ahb-raht-nah)* .... roundtrip, there and back
турист *(too-reest)* .... tourist
Туркменистан *(toork-men-ee-stahn)* .... Turkmenistan
туркмен *(toork-myen)* .... Turkmenian
туфли *(too-flee)* .... shoes
тушёное *(toosh-yoh-nah-yeh)* .... stewed
тысяча *(tih-syah-chah)* .... one thousand
тысячи *(tih-syah-chee)* .... one thousand
тысяч *(tih-syahch)* .... one thousand

У

у вас есть *(oo)(vahs)(yest)* .... you have
у вас есть? *(oo)(vahs)(yest)* .... Do you have?
у меня есть *(oo)(men-yah)(yest)* .... I have

у него есть *(oo)(nyeh-voh)(yest)* . . . . he has
у неё есть *(oo)(nyeh-yoh)(yest)* . . . . she has
у нас есть *(oo)(nahs)(yest)* . . . . we have
у них есть *(oo)(neehk)(yest)* . . . . they have
уезжать *(oo-yez-zhaht)* . . . . to leave
Узбекистан *(ooz-bek-ee-stahn)* . . . . Uzbekistan
узбек *(ooz-bek)* . . . . Uzbek
угол *(oog-ahl)* . . . . corner
углу *(oo-gloo)* . . . . corner
удачи *(oo-dah-chee)* . . . . good luck
ужин *(oo-zheen)* . . . . evening meal
укладывать *(oo-klah-dih-vaht)* . . . . to pack
Украина *(oo-krah-ee-nah)* . . . . Ukraine
украинец *(oo-krah-ee-nyets)* . . . . Ukrainian
улетает *(oo-lee-tah-yet)* . . . . (it) flies away
улица (ул.) *(oo-leet-sah)* . . . . street
умывальник *(oo-mih-vahl-neek)* . . . . washstand
универмаг *(oo-nee-vyair-mahg)* . . . . department store
универсальный магазин *(oo-nee-vyair-sahl-nee)(mah-gah-zeen)* .
. . . . department store
университет *(oo-nee-vyair-see-tyet)* . . . . university
уступите дорогу *(oo-stoo-peet-yeh)(dah-roh-goo)* . yield right of way
утро *(oo-trah)* . . . . morning
утра *(oo-trah)* . . . . morning
утром *(oo-trahm)* . . . . morning
уходить *(oo-hah-deet)* . . . . to leave (on foot)

Ф

факс *(fahks)* . . . . fax, facsimile
фарфор *(far-for)* . . . . china
Фаренгейт *(fah-ren-gate)* . . . . Fahrenheit
фаршированный *(far-shee-roh-vah-nee)* . . . . stuffed
февраль *(fyev-rahl)* . . . . February
фильм *(feelm)* . . . . film
фотоаппарат *(foh-tah-ahp-pah-raht)* . . . . camera
фотограф *(fah-toh-grahf)* . . . . photographer
фотоплёнка *(foh-tah-plyohn-kah)* . . . . film
фототовары *(foh-tah-tah-vah-rih)* . . . . camera supplies
Франция *(frahn-tsee-yah)* . . . . France
по-французски *(pah-frahn-tsoo-skee)* . . . . in French
фри *(free)* . . . . fried
фрукт *(frookt)* . . . . fruit
футбол *(foot-bohl)* . . . . soccer, football

X

химчистка *(heem-cheest-kah)* . . . . dry cleaners
хлеб *(hlyeb)* . . . . bread
ходит *(hoh-deet)* . . . . goes
холодильник *(hah-lah-deel-neek)* . . . . refrigerator
холодная *(hah-lohd-nah-yah)* . . . . cold
холодно *(hoh-lahd-nah)* . . . . cold
хорошая *(hah-roh-shah-yah)* . . . . good
хорошая погода *(hah-roh-shah-yah)(pah-go-dah)* . . good weather
хорошо сидит *(hah-rah-shoh)(see-deet)* . . . . it fits well
хотим *(hah-teem)* . . . . (we) would like
хотите *(hah-teet-yeh)* . . . . (you) would like
хочу *(hah-choo)* . . . . (I) would like
я хочу есть *(yah)(hah-choo)(yest)* . . . . I am hungry
я хочу купить *(yah)(hah-choo)(koo-peet)* . . . . . . I would like to buy
я хочу пить *(yah)(hah-choo)(peet)* . . . . I am thirsty
хрусталь *(hkroos-tahl)* . . . . crystal

Ц

царь *(tsar)* . . . . czar, tsar
цвет *(tsvet)* . . . . color
цвета *(tsvet-ah)* . . . . colors
цветок *(tsvet-ohk)* . . . . flower
цветы *(tsvet-ih)* . . . . flowers
Цельсий *(tsel-see)* . . . . Celsius
цена *(tsyen-ah)* . . . . price
цене *(tsyen-yeh)* . . . . price
цены *(tsyen-ih)* . . . . prices
центр *(tsen-ter)* . . . . city center
центра *(tsen-trah)* . . . . center
церквей *(tsair-kvay)* . . . . churches
цирк *(tseerk)* . . . . circus

Ч

чай *(chy)* . . . . tea
чая *(chah-yah)* . . . . tea

час *(chahs)* . . . . o'clock, hour
который час? *(kah-toh-ree)(chahs)* . . . . what time is it?
часов *(chah-sohv)* . . . . o'clock
часто *(chah-stah)* . . . . often
часы *(chah-sih)* . . . . clock, watch, watchmaker
часах *(chah-sahk)* . . . . clocks, watches
чашка *(chahsh-kah)* . . . . cup
чашки *(chahsh-kee)* . . . . cups
чашку *(chahsh-koo)* . . . . cup
чемодан *(cheh-mah-dahn)* . . . . suitcase
четверть *(chet-virt)* . . . . a quarter (toward)
без четверти *(byez)(chet-virt-ee)* . . . . a quarter from
четверг *(chet-vyairg)* . . . . Thursday
четыре *(cheh-tir-ee)* . . . . four
четырнадцать *(cheh-tir-nud-tset)* . . . . fourteen
чёрный *(chyor-nee)* . . . . black
Чили *(chee-lee)* . . . . Chile
числа *(chee-slah)* . . . . numbers
число *(chee-sloh)* . . . . number
читать *(chee-taht)* . . . . to read
что *(shtoh)* . . . . what, that
чулки *(chool-kee)* . . . . stockings

Ш

шарф *(sharf)* . . . . scarf
Швеция *(shvet-see-yah)* . . . . Sweden
шесть *(shest)* . . . . six
шестнадцать *(shest-nahd-tset)* . . . . sixteen
шестьдесят *(shest-dyes-yaht)* . . . . sixty
шкатулка *(shkah-tool-kah)* . . . . lacquer box
шкаф *(shkahf)* . . . . wardrobe, cupboard
школа *(shkohl-ah)* . . . . school
школе *(shkohl-yeh)* . . . . school
шляпа *(shlyah-pah)* . . . . hat
шорты *(shohr-tih)* . . . . shorts
шоссе *(shahs-syeh)* . . . . main road
штат *(shtaht)* . . . . state
шторм *(shtorm)* . . . . storm

Э

экватор *(ek-vah-tar)* . . . . equator
экзамен *(ek-zah-myen)* . . . . exam
экономика *(ek-ah-noh-mee-kah)* . . . . economics
экспресс *(ek-spres)* . . . . express
электроприборы *(el-ek-troh-pree-bohr-ih)* . . . . electrical goods
электрички *(el-ek-treech-kee)* . . . . suburban trains
эра *(air-ah)* . . . . era
эскалатор *(es-kah-lah-tor)* . . . . escalator
Эстония *(es-toh-nee-yah)* . . . . Estonia
эстонец *(es-toh-nyets)* . . . . Estonian
этаж *(eh-tahzh)* . . . . floor (of building)
это / этой / эту *(et-tah)/(et-toy)/(et-too)* . . . . . . that, this
это всё *(et-tah)(vsyoh)* . . . . that's all
эти / этими *(et-tee)/(et-tee-mee)* . . . . these
этого *(et-tah-vah)* . . . . that

Ю

ювелирные изделия *(yoo-vee-leer-nee)(eez-dyeh-lee-yah)* . . . jewelry
юбка *(yoob-kah)* . . . . skirt
юг *(yoog)* . . . . south
Южная Америка *(yoozh-nah-yah)(ah-myeh-ree-kah)* . . . .
. . . . South America
Южная Африка *(yoozh-nah-yah)(ah-free-kah)* . . . . . . South Africa
Южная Дакота *(yoozh-nah-yah)(dah-koh-tah)* . . . . . . South Dakota
Южная Каролина *(yoozh-nah-yah)(kah-rah-lee-nah)* . . . .
. . . . South Carolina
юрта *(yoor-tah)* . . . . yurt

Я

я *(yah)* I
я хочу есть *(yah)(hah-choo)(yest)* . . . . I am hungry
я хочу пить *(yah)(hah-choo)(peet)* . . . . I am thirsty
яблоко *(yah-blah-kah)* . . . . apple
яблок *(yah-blahk)* . . . . apples
язык *(yah-zik)* . . . . language, tongue
яйца *(yight-sah)* . . . . eggs
январь *(yahn-var)* . . . . January
январе *(yahn-var-yeh)* . . . . January
Япония *(yah-pohn-ee-yah)* . . . . Japan
яхта *(yahk-tah)* . . . . yacht

This beverage guide is intended to explain the variety of beverages available to you while **в России**. It is by no means complete. Some of the experimenting has been left up to you, but this should get you started.

ГОРЯЧИЕ НАПИТКИ (hot drinks)

кофе	coffee
кофе с молоком	coffee with milk
чёрный кофе	black coffee
кофе по-восточному	Turkish coffee
какао	cocoa

чай с лимоном	tea with lemon
чай с вареньем	tea with jam
чай с молоком	tea with milk
чай с мёдом	tea with honey

Чай was traditionally made in a **самовар**. A very strong tea was made in a teapot which was kept warm on top of the samovar. A small portion of the tea was poured into a cup and diluted with hot water from the samovar.

ФРУКТОВЫЙ СОК (fruit juice)

Don't miss a chance to sample Russian fruit juices. They are delicious. You'll find juice bars in the larger grocery stores.

апельсиновый сок	orange juice
яблочный сок	apple juice
виноградный сок	grape juice
клюквенный морс	cranberry juice
сливовый сок	prune juice
абрикосовый сок	apricot juice
персиковый сок	peach juice
томатный сок	tomato juice

ХОЛОДНЫЕ НАПИТКИ (cold drinks)

молоко	milk
фруктовый коктейль	milkshake
кефир	sour-milk drink
ряженка	thick, sour milk
кисель	sour-fruit drink
лимонад	lemonade
"Байкал"	cola drink
минеральная вода	mineral water
квас	kvass

ПИВО (beer)

If you are visiting during the summer, you'll want to visit the streetside beer stalls.

светлое пиво	light beer
тёмное пиво	dark beer

ВИНО (wine)

красное вино	red wine
белое вино	white wine
розовое вино	rosé wine
вермут	vermouth
портвейн	port
херес	sherry
шампанское	champagne

СПИРТНЫЕ НАПИТКИ (alcohol)

Both **спиртные напитки** and **вино** can be purchased by the bottle or by weight. A shot is 50 grams and a glass of wine is approximately 150 grams.

водка	vodka
виски	whisky
джин	gin
ром	rum
аперитив	aperitif
ликёр	liqueur
коньяк	cognac
лёд	ice
со льдом	with ice

Меню
menu

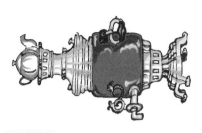

Завтрак? Обед? Ужин?

отварное	boiled
жареное	roasted, fried
тушёное	stewed
запечённое	baked
фаршированный	stuffed
на вертеле	grilled on a rotisserie
паровой	steamed

Что мне нужно? (What do I need?)

масло	butter
сахар	sugar
варенье	jam
мёд	honey
соль	salt
перец	pepper
уксус	vinegar
растительное масло	oil
оливковое масло	olive oil
горчица	mustard
соус	sauce, gravy
сыр	cheese
вода	water
лёд	ice
майонез	mayonnaise
сметана	sour cream
кефир	kefir; soured milk
творог	farmer's cheese
йогурт	yogurt

FOLD HERE

Овощи (vegetables)

баклажаны	eggplant
горох	peas
грибы	mushrooms
капуста	cabbage
красная капуста	red cabbage
цветная капуста	cauliflower
картофель	potatoes
кукуруза	corn
лук	onions
морковь	carrots
перец	pepper / green pepper
перец горький	pimentos
помидоры	tomatoes
редиска	radishes
репа	turnips
свёкла	beets
шпинат	spinach

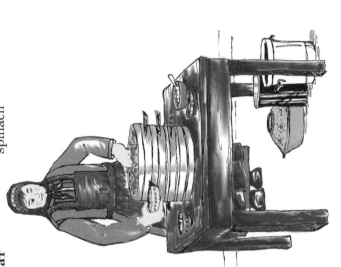

(pree-yaht-nah-vah) (ah-peh-tee-tah)

Приятного аппетита!

FOLD HERE

Десерт (dessert)

мороженое	ice cream
ванильное мороженое	vanilla ice cream
шоколадное мороженое	chocolate ice cream
кисель	jello-style dessert
компот	compote
крем	cream
взбитые сливки	whipped cream
рисовый пудинг	rice pudding
шоколадный соус	chocolate sauce
торт	torte, cake
кекс	muffin, spongecake
пирог, печенье	pie, cake, tart
пряники	pastries, honeycake
пирожные	cake

Фрукты (fruit)

апельсин	orange
арбуз	watermelon
банан	banana
виноград	grapes
вишня	cherries
грейпфрут	grapefruit
груша	pear
дыня	melon
клубника	strawberries
лимон	lemon
малина	raspberries
персик	peach
яблоко	apple
ягоды	berries

Птица и дичь (poultry and game)

курица/цыплёнок	chicken
гусь	goose
утка	duck
индейка	turkey
куропатка	partridge
вальдшнеп	woodcock
перепел	quail
кролик	rabbit
оленина	venison

Закуски (appetizers)

икра	caviar
красная икра	red caviar
чёрная икра	black caviar
сардины	sardines
сельдь	herring
креветки	shrimp
балык	smoked sturgeon
сосиски	sausages
колбаса	cold cuts
паштет	pâté
форшмак	potato-and-meat hash
бутерброды открытые	open-faced sandwiches
бутерброды закрытые	sandwiches

Хлеб (bread and dough dishes)

чёрный хлеб	black / rye bread
ржаной хлеб	black / rye bread
белый хлеб	white / wheat bread
пшеничный хлеб	white / wheat bread
булочки	rolls
блины	pancakes, blinis
пельмени	stuffed dumplings
каша	hot cereal
манная	farina
пирожки	small meat or cabbage pies
кулебяка	breaded fish or meat loaf
пирог	pie filled with meat or vegetables
рис	rice
нон	flatbread
самса	baked, stuffed puff pastry
лагман	long, stout noodles
манты	steamed dumplings

Яйца (eggs)

яйца вкрутую	hard-boiled eggs
яйца всмятку	soft-boiled eggs
яичница	fried eggs
взбитая яичница	scrambled eggs
фаршированные яйца	stuffed eggs
яйца с икрой	eggs with caviar

Суп (soup)

борщ	borsch
щи	cabbage or sauerkraut soup
шурпа	broth with vegetables
уха	fish soup
лапша	noodle soup
молочная лапша	milk soup with noodles
суп грибной	mushroom soup
суп овощной	vegetable soup
харчо	Georgian mutton and rice soup
шурпа	Uzbek mutton, bean and tomato soup
суп картофельный	potato soup
суп гороховый	pea soup
солянка	spicy, thick soup
бульон	bouillon
бульон с яйцом	bouillon with an egg
бульон с фрикадельками	bouillon with meatballs

Рыба (fish dishes)

треска	cod
камбала	flounder
карп	carp
лосось	salmon
кета	Siberian salmon
щука	pike
раки	crayfish
краб	crab
окунь	perch
судак	pike perch
палтус	halibut
форель	trout
осетрина	sturgeon

Мясо (meat dishes)

баранина	mutton
ветчина	ham
говядина	beef
свинина	pork
телятина	veal
бараньи котлеты	lamb chops
ветчина жареная	fried ham
колбаса жареная	fried sausages
телятина жареная	roast veal
ростбиф	roast beef
поджарка	roast pork
бефстроганов	beef stroganoff
бифштекс	beefsteak
рагу	stew
рулет	meatloaf
гуляш	goulash
котлеты	chopped beef
шашлык	shashlik, kebabs
долма	stuffed grape leaves
голубцы мясные	stuffed cabbage
язык	tongue
печёнка	liver
бекон	bacon
битки/биточки	meatballs
купаты	spicy pork sausage
плов	pilaf

Салат (salad)

салат из фруктов	fruit salad
салат из огурцов	cucumber salad
салат из помидоров	tomato salad
салат из фасоли	bean salad
салат из редиса	radish salad
салат картофельный	potato salad
салат из белых грибов	white-mushroom salad
салат "столичный"	meat-and-vegetable salad
винегрет	beets and other vegetables

(yah)
я

(ohn)
он

(ah-nah)
она

(mwee)
мы

(vwee)
вы

(ah-nee)
они

(zah-kah-zih-vaht)
заказывать

(yah) *(zah-kah-zih-vah-yoo)*
я заказываю

(pah-koo-paht)
покупать

(yah) *(pah-koo-pah-yoo)*
я покупаю

(ee-zoo-chaht)
изучать

(yah) *(ee-zoo-chah-yoo)*
я изучаю

(pahv-tar-yaht)
повторять

(yah) *(pahv-tar-yah-yoo)*
я повторяю

(pah-nee-maht)
понимать

(yah) *(pah-nee-mah-yoo)*
я понимаю

(gah-vah-reet)
говорить

(yah) *(gah-vah-ryoo)*
я говорю

he	I
we	she
they	you
to buy	to order / reserve
I buy	I order / I reserve
to repeat	to learn
I repeat	I learn
to speak / say	to understand
I speak / I say	I understand

(yek-haht)
ехать

(yah) (yeh-doo)
я еду

(pree-yez-zhaht)
приезжать

(yah) (pree-yez-zhy-yoo)
я приезжаю

(vee-dyet)
видеть

(yah) (vee-zhoo)
я вижу

(zheet)
жить

(yah) (zhee-voo)
я живу

(zhdaht)
ждать

(yah) (zhdoo)
я жду

(ees-kaht)
искать

(yah) (eesh-choo)
я ищу

(yest)
есть

(yah) (yem)
я ем

(peet)
пить

(yah) (pyoo)
я пью

(yah) (hah-choo)
я хочу . . .

(men-yeh) (noozh-nah)
мне нужно . . .

(men-yah) (zah-voot)
меня зовут . . .

(oo) (men-yah) (yest)
у меня есть . . .

to arrive	to go (by vehicle)
I arrive	I go (by vehicle)
to live / reside	to see
I live / I reside	I see
to look for	to wait for
I look for	I wait for
to drink	to eat
I drink	I eat
I need . . .	I would like . . .
I have . . .	my name is . . .

(prah-dah-vaht)
продавать
(yah) *(prah-dah-yoo)*
я продаю

(pah-sih-laht)
посылать
(yah) *(pah-sih-lah-yoo)*
я посылаю

(spaht)
спать
(yah) *(splyoo)*
я сплю

(zvah-neet)
звонить
(yah) *(zvah-nyoo)*
я звоню

(die-tee) *(men-yeh)*
дайте мне . . .

(pee-saht)
писать
(yah) *(pee-shoo)*
я пишу

(pah-kah-zih-vaht)
показывать
(yah) *(pah-kah-zih-vah-yoo)*
я показываю

(zah-plah-teet) *(zah)*
заплатить за
(yah) *(zah-plah-choo)* *(zah)*
я заплачу за

(znaht)
знать
(yah) *(znah-yoo)*
я знаю

(mohch)
мочь
(yah) *(mah-goo)*
я могу

(chee-taht)
читать
(yah) *(chee-tah-yoo)*
я читаю

(poot-yeh-shest-vah-vaht)
путешествовать
(yah) *(poot-yeh-shest-voo-yoo)*
я путешествую

to send

I send

to phone

I phone

to write

I write

to pay for

I pay for

to be able to / can

I am able to / I can

to travel

I travel

to sell

I sell

to sleep

I sleep

give me . . .

to show

I show

to know (fact)

I know (fact)

to read

I read

(lee-tyet)
лететь

(yah) *(lee-choo)*
я лечу

(oo-yez-zhaht)
уезжать

(yah) *(oo-yez-zhah-yoo)*
я уезжаю

(dyeh-laht)
делать

(yah) *(dyeh-lah-yoo)*
я делаю

(dyeh-laht) *(pyair-yeh-sahd-koo)*
делать пересадку

(yah) *(dyeh-lah-yoo)* *(pyair-yeh-sahd-koo)*
я делаю пересадку

(oo-klah-dih-vaht)
укладывать

(yah) *(oo-klah-dih-vah-yoo)*
я укладываю

(pree-hah-deet)
приходить

(poh-yezd) *(pree-hoh-deet)* *(vuh)*
Поезд приходит в …

(aht-hah-deet)
отходить

(poh-yezd) *(aht-hoh-deet)* *(vuh)*
Поезд отходит в …

(oo-hah-deet)
уходить

(yah) *(oo-hah-zhoo)*
я ухожу

(yek-haht) *(nah)* *(mah-shee-nyeh)*
ехать на машине

(yah) *(yeh-doo)* *(nah)* *(mah-shee-nyeh)*
я еду на машине

(stee-raht)
стирать

(yah) *(stee-rah-yoo)*
я стираю

(tyair-yaht)
терять

(yah) *(tyair-yah-yoo)*
я теряю

(zah-nee-maht)
занимать

(zah-nee-mah-yet)
занимает

to leave

I leave

to transfer

I transfer

to arrive (trains, etc.)

the train arrives at . . .

to leave (on foot)

I leave

to wash / clean (clothes)

I wash / I clean (clothes)

to occupy / take up

it occupies / it takes up

to fly

I fly

to make

I make

to pack

I pack

to depart (trains, etc.)

the train departs at ...

to drive

I drive

to lose

I lose

(kahk) *(dee-lah)*
Как дела?

(dah) *(svee-dahn-yah)*
До свидания!

(pah-zhahl-oos-tah)
пожалуйста

(eez-vee-neet-yeh)
извините

(spah-see-bah)
спасибо

(see-vohd-nyah)
сегодня

(zahv-trah)
завтра

(vchee-rah)
вчера

(skohl-kah) *(et-tah)* *(stoy-eet)*
Сколько это стоит?

(oo) *(vahs)* *(yest)*
У вас есть . . . ?

(aht-krih-tah) *(zah-krih-tah)*
открыто - закрыто

(bahl-shoy) *(mah-lyen-kee)*
большой-маленький

good bye!	How are things? / How are you?
excuse me	please / you're welcome
today	thank-you
yesterday	tomorrow
do you have . . .?	How much does this cost?
big - small	open - closed

(zdah-rohv) *(bohl-yen)* **здоров - болен**	*(hah-rah-shoh)* *(ploh-hah)* **хорошо - плохо**
(gor-yah-chah-yah) *(hah-lohd-nah-yah)* **горячая - холодная**	*(kah-roht-kah-yah)* *(dleen-nah-yah)* **короткая - длинная**
(vwee-soh-kah-yah) *(mah-lyen-kah-yah)* **высокая - маленькая**	*(nahd)* *(pohd)* **над - под**
(nah-lyev-ah) *(nah-prah-vah)* **налево - направо**	*(myed-lyen-nah)* *(bis-trah)* **медленно - быстро**
(stah-ree) *(mah-lah-doy)* **старый - молодой**	*(dah-rah-gah-yah)* *(dyeh-shyoh-vah-yah)* **дорогая - дешёвая**
(bah-gaht) *(byed-yen)* **богат - беден**	*(mnoh-gah)* *(mah-lah)* **много - мало**

good - bad	healthy - sick
short - long	hot - cold
above - below	tall / high - small
slow - fast	to the left - to the right
expensive - inexpensive	old - young
a lot - a little	rich - poor

Now that you've finished...

You've done it!

You've completed all the Steps, stuck your labels, flashed your cards, cut out your beverage and menu guides and practiced your new language. Do you realize how far you've come and how much you've learned? You've accomplished what it could take years to achieve in a traditional language class.

You can now confidently

- ask questions,
- understand directions,
- make reservations,
- order food and
- shop for anything.

And you can do it all in a foreign language! Go anywhere with confidence — from a large cosmopolitan restaurant to a small, out-of-the-way village where no one speaks English. Your experiences will be much more enjoyable and worry-free now that you speak the language.

As you've seen, learning a foreign language can be fun. Why limit yourself to just one? Now you're ready to learn another language with the *10 minutes a day®* Series!

Kris Kershul

Kristine Kershul

To place an order –

- Visit us at www.bbks.com, day or night.
- Call us at (800) 488-5068 or (206) 284-4211 between 8:00 a.m. and 5:00 p.m. Pacific Time, Monday - Friday.
- If you have questions about ordering, please call us. You may also fax us at (206) 284-3660 or email us at customer.service@bbks.com.

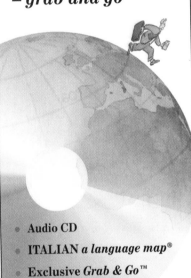